SCOTT FORESMAN · ADDISON WESLEY

Mathematics

Grade 5

Practice
Masters/Workbook

PEARSON

Scott
Foresman

Editorial Offices: Glenview, Illinois • Parsippany, New Jersey • New York, New York

Sales Offices: Parsippany, New Jersey • Duluth, Georgia • Glenview, Illinois
Coppell, Texas • Ontario, California • Mesa, Arizona

Overview

Practice Masters provide additional practice on the concept or concepts taught in each lesson.

ISBN 0-328-04957-3

4 5 6 7 8 9 10 V084 09 08 07 06 05 04

Place Value Through Billions

Write the word form for each number and tell the value of the underlined digit.

1. 34,23<u>5</u>,345 _____

_____

_____

2. 1<u>9</u>,673,890,004 _____

_____

_____

3. Write 2,430,090 in expanded form.

_____

Write each number in standard form.

4. 80,000,000 + 4,000,000 + 100 + 8 _____

5. twenty-nine billion, thirty-two million _____

6. **Number Sense** What number is 10,000 less than 337,676? _____

Test Prep

7. Which number is 164,502,423 decreased by 100,000?

   A. 164,402,423   **B.** 164,501,423   **C.** 164,512,423   **D.** 264,502,423

8. **Writing in Math** Explain how you would write 423,090,709,000 in word form.

_____

_____

_____

Comparing and Ordering Whole Numbers

Complete. Write >, <, or = for each $\bigcirc$.

1. 23,412 $\bigcirc$ 23,098   **2.** 9,000,000 $\bigcirc$ 9,421,090

Order these numbers from least to greatest.

3. 7,545,999 7,445,999 7,554,000

_____

4. Number Sense What digit could be in the ten millions place of a number that is less than 55,000,000 but greater than 25,000,000?   _____

5. Put the trenches in order from the least depth to the greatest depth.

Depths of Major Ocean Trenches

Trench	Depth (in feet)
Philippine Trench	32,995
Mariana Trench	35,840
Kermadec Trench	32,963
Tonga Trench	35,433

_____

_____

_____

_____

Test Prep

6. These numbers are ordered from greatest to least. Which number could be placed in the second position?

2,643,022 1,764,322 927,322

A. 2,743,022   **B.** 1,927,304   **C.** 1,443,322   **D.** 964,322

7. Writing in Math Explain why 42,678 is greater than 42,067.

_____

_____

_____

Place Value Through Thousandths

Write the word form for each number and tell the value of the underlined digit.

1. 4.34<u>5</u> _____

_____

2. 7.<u>8</u>80 _____

_____

Write each number in standard form.

3. 6 + 0.3 + 0.02 + 0.001   _____

4. seven and five hundred thirty-three thousandths   _____

Write two decimals that are equivalent to each number.

5. 0.68 _____

6. 0.9 _____

7. Number Sense Explain why 0.2 and 0.020 are not equivalent.

_____

_____

_____

8. Cheri's time in the bobsled race was 1 min, 38.29 sec.
Write the word form and the value of the 9 in Cheri's time.

_____

Test Prep

9. Which is the word form of the underlined digit in 46.<u>5</u>04?

   A. 5 ones   **B.** 5 tenths   **C.** 5 hundredths   **D.** 5 thousandths

10. Writing in Math Write the value for
each digit in the number 1.639.   _____

Comparing and Ordering Decimals

Write >, <, or = for each $\bigcirc$.

1. 5.424 $\bigcirc$ 5.343   **2.** 0.33 $\bigcirc$ 0.330   **3.** 9.489 $\bigcirc$ 9.479

4. 21.012 $\bigcirc$ 21.01   **5.** 223.21 $\bigcirc$ 223.199   **6.** 5.43 $\bigcirc$ 5.432

Order these numbers from least to greatest.

7. 8.37, 8.3, 8.219, 8.129   _____

8. 0.012, 0.100, 0.001, 0.101   _____

9. Number Sense Name three
numbers between 0.33 and 0.34.   _____

10. Which runner came in first place?

_____

Half Mile Run

Runner	Time (minutes)
Amanda	8.016
Calvin	7.049
Liz	7.03
Steve	8.16

11. Who ran faster, Amanda or Steve?

_____

12. Who ran for the longest time?

_____

Test Prep

13. Which number is less than 28.43?

A. 28.435   **B.** 28.34   **C.** 28.430   **D.** 29.43

14. Writing in Math Explain why it is not reasonable to say
that 4.23 is less than 4.13.

_____

_____

_____

Name_____

Place-Value Patterns

Tell how many *tens, hundreds,* and *thousands* are in each number.

1. 12,000 _____

_____

2. 9,000,000 _____

_____

What number makes each statement true?

3. $9,000 = 900 \times$ _____

4. $600,000 = 60 \times$ _____

5. $4 = 0.4 \times$ _____

6. $60 = 0.6 \times$ _____

Name each number in two different ways.

7. 90,000,000 _____

8. 40,000 _____

9. Number Sense How many thousands are in 5,000,000? _____

10. The volume of Fort Peck Dam is $96,050 \times 1,000$ m^3.
Suppose the state of Montana decides to increase the
volume of the dam. After the improvements, Fort Peck will
hold 10 times as many cubic meters. How many cubic
meters will Fort Peck hold after the improvements?

_____

Test Prep

11. Which is the correct product for $1,000 \times 0.4$?

A. 4,000   **B.** 400   **C.** 4.000   **D.** 0.0004

12. Writing in Math Complete the missing information in this
sentence:

Twenty-nine _____ is equal to $29 \times 1,000$.

PROBLEM-SOLVING SKILL
Read and Understand

The day a new manufacturing plant opened, the population of
Sunny Grove was 13,731 people. In its first year of operation,
2,950 new residents moved into Sunny Grove. In the second
year, double that number moved in. What was the population of
Sunny Grove by the end of the second year of
the plant's operation?

1. Tell the problem in your own words. _____

_____

_____

2. Identify key facts and details. _____

_____

_____

3. Tell what the question is asking. _____

_____

_____

4. Show the main idea.

5. Solve the problem. Write the answer in a complete sentence.

_____

_____

Name_____

Adding and Subtracting Mentally

Show how you can add or subtract mentally.

1. 70 + 90 + 30 = _____

2. 350 − 110 = _____

National Monuments

Name	State	Acres
George Washington Carver	Missouri	210
Navajo	Arizona	360
Fort Sumter	South Carolina	200
Russell Cave	Alabama	310

3. How many more acres are there at Navajo monument than at George Washington Carver monument?

_____

4. How many acres are there at Fort Sumter and Russell Cave combined?

_____

Test Prep

5. Fresh Market bought 56 lb of apples in August from a local orchard. In September, the market purchased an additional 52 lb of apples and 32 lb of strawberries. How many pounds of fruit did the market buy?

A. 108 lb   **B.** 140 lb   **C.** 150 lb   **D.** 240 lb

6. Writing in Math Write the definition and give an example of the Commutative Property of Addition.

_____

_____

Name_____

Rounding Whole Numbers and Decimals

Round each number to the place of the underlined digit.

1. 32.6̲0   _____

2. 48̲9,334,209 _____

3. 324̲,650   _____

4. 32.0̲73   _____

5. **Reasoning** Name two different numbers
   that round to 30 when rounded to the nearest ten. _____

In 2000, Italy produced 7,464,000 tons of wheat, and Pakistan
produced 21,079,000 tons of wheat. Round each country's wheat
production in metric tons to the nearest hundred thousand.

6. Italy   _____

7. Pakistan   _____

The price of wheat in 1997 was $3.38 per bushel. In 1998, the
price was $2.65 per bushel. Round the price per bushel of wheat
for each year to the nearest tenth of a dollar.

8. 1997 _____

9. 1998 _____

Test Prep

10. Which number rounds to 15,700,000 when rounded to the
    nearest hundred thousand?

    A. 15,000,000   **B.** 15,579,999   **C.** 15,649,999   **D.** 15,659,999

11. **Writing in Math** Write a definition of rounding in your own words.

_____

_____

Name_____

Estimating Sums and Differences

Estimate each sum or difference.

1. 5,602 − 2,344 _____

2. 7.4 + 3.1 + 9.8 _____

3. 2,314 + 671 _____

4. 54.23 − 2.39 _____

5. Number Sense Wesley estimated 5.82 − 4.21 to be about 2.
Is this an overestimate or an underestimate? Explain.

_____

_____

6. Estimate the total precipitation in inches and in days for Asheville and Wichita.

Average Yearly Precipitation of U.S. Cities

City	Inches	Days
Asheville, North Carolina	47.71	124
Wichita, Kansas	28.61	85

_____

7. In inches and in days, about how much more average yearly precipitation is there in Asheville than in Wichita?

_____

Test Prep

8. Which numbers should you add to estimate the answer to this problem:

87,087 + 98,000?

A. 88,000 + 98,000   **B.** 87,000 + 98,000

C. 85,000 + 95,000   **D.** 80,000 + 90,000

9. Writing in Math You want to estimate 5.25 − 3.3. Why would using front-end estimation and adjusting tell you more about the answer than rounding?

_____

_____

Name_____

Plan and Solve

Yarn Wade and his mother bought four colors of yarn at the craft store. The blue yarn was longer than the green yarn but shorter than the red yarn. The yellow yarn was shorter than the green yarn. Order the colored yarns from the shortest to the longest.

SHORTEST   LONGEST

●————————————●————————————●————————————●

yellow   red
yarn   yarn

_____   _____

1. Finish the picture to help solve the problem.

2. What strategy was used to solve the problem?

_____

_____

3. Write the answer to the problem in a complete sentence.

_____

_____

_____

Basketball Juanita's team is playing in a basketball competition. Each of the seven teams in the competition play all the other teams once. How many games are played in the competition?

4. What strategy did you use to solve this problem?

_____

5. Give the answer in a complete sentence.

_____

_____

Name_____

Adding and Subtracting Whole Numbers

Add or subtract.

1.
```
  29,543
+ 13,976
```

2.
```
  93,210
- 21,061
```

3.
```
  369,021
- 325,310
```

4.
```
  893,887
+  22,013
```

5. 971,234 + 55,423 = _____

6. **Number Sense** Is 4,000 a reasonable estimate for the difference of 9,215 − 5,022? Explain.

_____

7. How many people were employed as public officials and natural scientists?

_____

8. How many more people were employed as university teachers than as lawyers and judges?

_____

People Employed in U.S. by Occupation in 2000

Occupation	Workers
Public officials	753,000
Natural scientists	566,000
University teachers	961,000
Lawyers and judges	926,000

Test Prep

9. Which is the difference between 403,951 and 135,211?

   A. 200,000   **B.** 221,365   **C.** 268,740   **D.** 539,162

10. **Writing in Math** Issac is adding 59,029 and 55,678. Should his answer be greater than or less than 100,000? Explain how you know.

_____

_____

_____

Adding Decimals

Add.

1.	58.0	2.	40.5	3.	34.587	4.	43.1000
	+ 3.6		+ 22.3		+ 21.098		+ 8.4388

5. $16.036 + 7.009 =$ _____   6. $92.30 + 0.32 =$ _____

7. **Number Sense** Reilly adds 45.3 and 3.21. Should his sum be greater than or less than 48? Tell how you know.

_____

_____

_____

In science class, students weighed different amounts of tin. Carmen weighed 4.361 g, Kim weighed 2.704 g, Simon weighed 5.295 g, and Angelica weighed 8.537 g.

8. How many grams of tin did Carmen and Angelica have combined?

_____

9. How many grams of tin did Kim and Simon have combined?

_____

Test Prep

10. In December the snowfall was 0.03 in. and in January it was 2.1 in. Which was the total snowfall?

   A. 3.2 in.   **B.** 2.40 in.   **C.** 2.13 in.   **D.** 0.03 in.

11. **Writing in Math** Explain why it is important to line up decimal numbers by their place value when you add or subtract them.

_____

_____

Name_____

Subtracting Decimals

Subtract.

1.   92.1
       − 32.6
       _____

2.   52.7
       − 36.9
       _____

3.   85.76
       − 12.986
       _____

4.   32.7
       − 2.328
       _____

5. 8.7 − 0.3 = _____

6. 23.3 − 1.32 = _____

7. Number Sense Kelly subtracted 2.3 from 20 and got 17.7.
Explain why this answer is reasonable.

_____

_____

At a local swim meet, the second place swimmer of the
100 m freestyle had a time of 9.33 sec. The first place
swimmer's time was 1.32 sec faster than the second place
swimmer. The third place time was 13.65 sec.

8. What was the time for the first place swimmer?   _____

9. What was the difference in time between
the second and third place swimmers?   _____

Test Prep

10. Miami's annual precipitation in 2000 was 61.05 in. Albany's was
46.92 in. How much greater was Miami's rainfall than Albany's?

A. 107.97 in.   **B.** 54.31 in.   **C.** 14.93 in.   **D.** 14.13 in.

11. Writing in Math Explain how to subtract 7.6 from 20.39.

_____

_____

_____

Name_____

Look Back and Check

Art Collection The Collector's Museum is home to lots of great art. The most valuable item is a painting finished in 1840 called *The Mirror.* Its estimated value is $1,202,450. The piece titled *A Summer Memory* is valued at $100,000 less than the value of *The Mirror.* The entire art collection is estimated to be worth $13,000,000. Overall there are 45 works of art in the museum. What is the total estimated value of the other 43 works of art?

Jacques solved the Art Collection problem. Check his work.

	Jacques
$13,000,000	
$1,202,450	?

$13,000,000 – $1,202,450 = $11,797,550
The 43 works of art are worth $11,797,550.

1. Did Jacques answer the right question? Explain.

_____

_____

2. Is his answer correct? Explain.

_____

_____

_____

Solve the problem. Then, look back and check your work.

3. An empty jar weighs 39 g. A jar that is full of water weighs 207 g. What does the water in the jar weigh?

_____

Name_____

Champions

At a gymnastics meet, Karl took first place. Karl scored 9.836
on the vault, Yao received a score of 9.772 on the parallel bars,
and Quincy scored 9.672 on the vault.

1. How much higher was Karl's vault
   score than Quincy's vault score?   _____

2. What information did you not need to answer the question?

   _____

   _____

Four weight lifters competed in the state tournament. Barney
lifted 205 kg, Eddie lifted 290 kg, Pierre lifted 305 kg, and
Nathan lifted 325 kg.

3. How much more did Eddie lift than Barney?   _____

4. How much more did Eddie and Pierre lift
   combined than Barney and Nathan combined?   _____

Six runners competed in a race. Kathryn finished third. Salma
finished ahead of Kathryn and Marita. Jackie finished before
Lara but after Nikki. List the runners in the order they finished.

5. Draw a picture to help you solve the problem.

6. Write your answer in a complete sentence.

   _____

   _____

Multiplication Patterns

Find each product. Use patterns and properties to compute mentally.

1. $40 \times 20 =$

2. $50 \times 700 =$

3. $20 \times 2 \times 30 =$

_____

_____

_____

4. $2 \times 50 \times 30 =$

5. $250 \times 37 \times 4 =$

6. $20 \times 65 \times 5 =$

_____

_____

_____

7. How many calories are in 10 peaches?

_____

8. How many calories are in 5 apples?

_____

Calories in Fruit

Fruit (1 piece)	Calories
Apple	80
Orange	60
Peach	35

9. Callie ate 3 oranges each day for 10 days.
How many calories did all of these oranges have? _____

10. Algebra $m \times n = 6{,}300$. If m and n are 2-digit multiples of
10, what numbers could m and n be?

_____

Test Prep

11. Which of the following has a product of 1,600?

A. $4{,}000 \times 400$ **B.** 4×400 **C.** 400×400 **D.** 40×400

12. Writing in Math Write a definition for the Associative
Property of Multiplication in your own words and explain
how you would use it to compute $4 \times 27 \times 25$ mentally.

_____

_____

_____

Name_____

Estimating Products

Estimate each product.

1. $36 \times 12 \times 9 =$ _____

2. $16 \times 7 \times 34 =$ _____

3. $2 \times 82 \times 26 =$ _____

4. $56 \times 11 \times 2 =$ _____

5. $44 \times 67 \times 7 =$ _____

6. $22 \times 69 \times 4 =$ _____

7. $53 \times 78 \times 21 =$ _____

8. $6 \times 12 \times 42 =$ _____

9. Number Sense Give three numbers whose product is about 9,000. _____

10. About how much would it cost to buy 4 CD/MP3 players and 3 MP3 players?

_____

Electronics Prices	
CD player	$74.00
MP3 player	$99.00
CD/MP3 player	$199.00
AM/FM radio	$29.00

11. Estimate to decide whether 8 AM/FM radios or 3 CD players cost less. Explain.

_____

_____

_____

Test Prep

12. Which is the closest estimate for the product of $2 \times 15 \times 5$?

A. 1,150   **B.** 150   **C.** 125   **D.** 50

13. Writing in Math Explain how you know whether an estimate of a product is an overestimate or an underestimate.

_____

_____

_____

Name_____

Mental Math:
Using the Distributive Property

Use the Distributive Property to multiply mentally.

1. $5 \times 607 =$ _____

2. $16 \times 102 =$ _____

3. $7 \times 420 =$ _____

4. $265 \times 5 =$ _____

5. $44 \times 60 =$ _____

6. $220 \times 19 =$ _____

7. $45 \times 280 =$ _____

8. $341 \times 32 =$ _____

9. Number Sense Fill in the blanks to show how the Distributive Property can be used to find 10×147.

$10 \times (150 - 3) = (10 \times 150) - ($ _____ $\times 3) =$

$1,500 -$ _____ $=$ _____

10. In 1990, there were 1,133 tornadoes in the U.S. If there were the same number of tornadoes for the next 10 years, what would have been the 10-year total?   _____

11. There were 1,071 tornadoes in the U.S. in 2000. What is the number of tornadoes multiplied by 20?   _____

Test Prep

12. If $4 \times 312 = (4 \times (300 + n)$, which is the value of n?

A. 4   **B.** 12   **C.** 48   **D.** 300

13. Writing in Math Margaret said that she used the Distributive Property to solve 4×444. Is her answer shown below correct? Explain.

$4 \times 444 = 4 \times (400 + 40 + 4) =$

$(4 \times 400) + (4 \times 40) + (4 \times 4) =$

$1,600 + 160 + 16 = 1,776$

_____

Name_____

Multiplying Whole Numbers

Find each product. Estimate to check that your answer is reasonable.

1. $543 \times 4 =$ _____

2. $254 \times 6 =$ _____

3. $756 \times 6 =$ _____

4. $560 \times 34 =$ _____

5. $424 \times 76 =$ _____

6. $513 \times 13 =$ _____

7. $107 \times 51 =$ _____

8. $816 \times 52 =$ _____

9.	**10.**	**11.**	**12.**	**13.**
15	876	55	89	235
$\times$ 29	$\times$ 4	$\times$ 44	$\times$ 65	$\times$ 32

14. Show how you can use the distributive property to multiply 22×85.

_____

15. Player A's longest home run distance is 484 ft. If Player A hits 45 home runs at his longest distance, what would the total distance be?

16. Player B's longest home run distance is 500 ft. There are 5,280 ft in 1 mi. How many home runs would Player B need to hit at his longest distance for the total to be greater than 1 mi?

Test Prep

17. Which is a reasonable answer for the product of $96 \times 7 \times 34$?

A. 672   **B.** 3,264   **C.** 22,848   **D.** 28,800

18. **Writing in Math** Why is 2,482 not a reasonable answer for 542×6?

_____

_____

_____

Choose a Calculation Method

Find each product. Tell what computation method you used.

1. $200 \times 50 =$ _____

2. $57 \times 7 =$ _____

3. $34 \times 22 =$ _____

4. $60 \times 17 =$ _____

5. $455 \times 309 =$ _____

6. $250 \times 200 =$ _____

7. **Number Sense** Find 77×96. Explain the method you used.

_____

_____

8. If Reneé rode her bicycle every day last year
for 7 mi each day, how many miles did she
ride altogether?   _____

9. Jason went to school 180 days last year.
If he walked 2 mi each way, how many miles
did he walk to and from school in all?   _____

Test Prep

10. Eli used mental math to solve 6×32. Which answer shows
how he could find the correct solution?

   A. $(3 \times 3) + (6 \times 2)$ **B.** $6 \times (9 \times 4)$

   C. $(6 \times 30) + (6 \times 2)$ **D.** $(6 \times 30) + 2$

11. **Writing in Math** Explain why mental math would not be
the best way to multiply 309×399.

_____

Name_____

Make an Organized List

Solve each problem. Write the answer in a complete sentence.

1. The mystery first name of a student in class does not begin
   with A, B, C, D, E, or F. The name's first letter comes before
   S, T, U, V, and W. The students whose names start with J,
   K, L, M, and N are not it. All letters from O through Q are
   not it. X, Y, Z and G, H, I are not it. What is the first letter of
   the mystery name?

   _____

   _____

2. Evan is thinking of a 3-digit odd number that uses the digit 7
   twice. The digit in the tens place is less than one. What is
   the number?

   _____

   _____

3. In the Laser Bowl Tournament, the judges take away
   50 points for a gutter ball. Players score 30 points for a red
   head pin strike, 20 points for a blue pin strike, and 15 points
   for a green pin strike. Two red head pin strikes in a row earns
   a one-time bonus of 50 points. How many points would you
   score if you earned 2 red head pin strikes in a row, 2 blue pin
   strikes, 0 green pin strikes, and 2 gutter balls?

   _____

4. **Writing in Math** Explain how you completed the list in
   Exercise 1.

   _____

   _____

   _____

Name_____

Decimal Patterns

Find each product. Use mental math.

1. $0.31 \times 10 =$

2. $100 \times 7.000 =$

3. $0.02 \times 1,000 =$

_____

_____

_____

4. $1,000 \times 5.1 =$

5. $45.6 \times 100 =$

6. $30.3 \times 1,000 =$

_____

_____

_____

7. $10 \times 102.2 =$

8. $100 \times 0.312 =$

9. $10 \times 7.522 =$

_____

_____

_____

10. $0.002 \times 10 =$

11. $578.31 \times 100 =$

12. $9.50 \times 1,000 =$

_____

_____

_____

13. Which student will enlarge her art to 5 mm if she enlarges it 100 times?

Student	Art Size
Jade	0.25 mm
Willa	0.24 mm
Jess	0.05 mm
Mae	0.37 mm

_____

14. How many millimeters will Mae's art be if she enlarges it 100 times?

_____

15. Algebra What is the value of n if $23.2 \times n = 2,320$? _____

Test Prep

16. Which is the product of 0.225×100?

A. 2.25   **B.** 22.5   **C.** 225   **D.** 2,250

17. Writing in Math Write a word problem using the number sentence $4.23 \times 10 = 42.3$.

_____

_____

Name_____

Estimating Decimal Products

Estimate each product.

1. $43 \times 2.1 =$ **2.** $5.40 \times 7 =$ **3.** $2.23 \times 15.9 =$

_____   _____   _____

4. $250 \times 5.1 =$ **5.** $0.02 \times 96 =$ **6.** $2.65 \times 7.4 =$

_____   _____   _____

7. $435.22 \times 2 =$ **8.** $781.93 \times 13 =$ **9.** $1.90 \times 526.8 =$

_____   _____   _____

10. James has $65 to spend at the clothing sale. Does James have enough money to buy one of each item?

Clothing Sale	
Sweater	$19.99
Pants	$29.99
Shirt	$12.99
Socks (1 pair)	$2.99

_____

_____

_____

11. Algebra A reasonable estimate for n is 1,000. Complete the problem to make it true.

$n \times$ _____ $= 6,350$

Test Prep

12. Which is a reasonable estimate for 41.3×8.78?

    A. 36   **B.** 360   **C.** 3,600   **D.** 36,000

13. Writing in Math Explain how you know that 200 is not a reasonable estimate for 19.6×20.

_____

_____

Multiplying Whole Numbers and Decimals

Find each product.

1. 5.4	**2.** 3.8	**3.** 0.55	**4.** 8.19
$\times\ \ 3$	$\times\ \ 4$	$\times\ \ \ \ 8$	$\times\ \ \ \ 5$

Insert a decimal point in each answer to make the equation true.

5. $5 \times 6.3 = 315$ _____

6. $3.001 \times 9 = 27009$ _____

7. Which desert accumulates the least amount of rain in August?

_____

8. If each month in Reno had the same average rainfall as in August, what would the total number of millimeters be after 12 months?

_____

Average Desert Rainfall in August

Reno	0.19 mm
Sahara	0.17 mm
Mojave	0.1 mm
Tempe	0.24 mm

Test Prep

9. Algebra If $4n = 3.60$, which is the value of n?

A. 0.09　　　　**B.** 0.9　　　　**C.** 9　　　　**D.** 90

Use the desert rainfall table to answer Exercise 10.

10. Writing in Math In December, the average rainfall in all of the deserts is 0.89 mm. Use the figures from the table to write a comparison of average desert rainfall in August and December.

_____

_____

_____

Using Grids to Multiply Decimals by Decimals

Write a multiplication sentence that describes the shaded areas of each grid.

1.

_____

2.

_____

Find each product. You can use 10 × 10 grids to help.

3. $0.3 \times 0.4 =$ _____

4. $0.2 \times 0.7 =$ _____

5. $0.6 \times 0.6 =$ _____

6. $0.5 \times 0.5 =$ _____

7. $0.7 \times 0.8 =$ _____

8. $0.6 \times 0.3 =$ _____

9. Write two numbers whose product is 0.56.

_____

10. Number Sense Is 0.4×0.8 greater than or less than 0.3×0.9?

_____

Test Prep

11. Which 10 × 10 grid shows the product of 0.6×0.2?

A.   **B.**   **C.**   **D.**

12. Writing in Math Explain why 0.2×0.4 equals 0.08 and not 0.8.

_____

_____

_____

_____

Multiplying Decimals by Decimals

Find each product.

1.	3.7 × 0.3	2.	4.4 × 0.2	3.	0.61 × 6.8	4.	1.9 × 0.005

5. $0.61 \times 6.8 =$ _____

6. $0.79 \times 0.005 =$ _____

Insert a decimal point in each answer to make the equation true.

7. $0.2 \times 4.4 = 088$ _____

8. $8.81 \times 5.2 = 45812$ _____

9. **Number Sense** The product of 4.7 and 6.5 equals 30.55.
What is the product of 4.7 and 0.65? 4.7 and 65?

_____   _____

10. What is the gravity in relation to Earth
that is 3.4 times the gravity of Mercury?

_____

11. What is the product of the gravity of Pluto
and Neptune?

_____

**Relative (to Earth)
Surface Gravity**

Planet	Gravity
Mercury	0.37
Neptune	1.22
Pluto	0.06

Test Prep

12. How many decimal places are in the product of a number
with decimal places to the thousandths multiplied by a
number with decimal places to the hundredths?

A. 2   **B.** 3   **C.** 4   **D.** 5

13. **Writing in Math** Explain how you know the number of
decimal places that should be in the product when you
multiply two decimal numbers together.

_____

Variables and Expressions

1. Write an algebraic expression to represent the cost of a concert ticket, *h*, with a service charge of $6.75.

_____

2. Write an algebraic expression to represent the cost of *m* gallons of gasoline if each gallon costs $1.45.

_____

Evaluate each expression for *n* = 3 and *n* = 6.

3. $0.2 \times n$ _____ _____

4. $n - 2.1$ _____ _____

5. $\frac{12}{n}$ _____ _____

6. $35 + n$ _____ _____

Complete each table.

7.

n	0.9 + *n*
0.5	
0.2	
0.15	
0.1	

8.

n	96 ÷ *n*
1	
2	
3	
4	

9. **Representations** What is another way to write the expression 44*n*? 44 ÷ *n*?

_____

Test Prep

10. Which is the correct product of *n* × 7 if *n* = $0.25?

   A. $3.25   **B.** $2.75   **C.** $2.25   **D.** $1.75

11. **Writing in Math** Write a situation that can be represented by the algebraic expression $3.25*d*.

_____

Name_____

Translating Words into Expressions

Write each word phrase an as algebraic expression.

1. the product of 5 and n _____

2. a height divided by 3 _____

3. $200 less than n _____

4. a number of books plus 30 _____

5. **Number Sense** Explain what the expression $6x$ means.

_____

_____

6. Dan is 12 in. taller than Jay. Use x for Jay's height. Which expression shows Dan's height, $x + 12$, $x - 12$, or $12x$? _____

7. There are 60 min in a hour. If there are y hr in a day, what expression shows the number of minutes in a day, $60y$, $60 + y$, or $\frac{y}{60}$? _____

8. Write two word phrases for the expression $\frac{t}{30}$.

_____

_____

9. **Writing in Math** Explain the difference between the expressions $x - 3$ and $3 - x$.

_____

_____

_____

Find a Rule

Find a rule for each table. Write the rule in words.

1.

Input	Output
6	18
24	36
48	60
72	84

_____

2.

Input	Output
5	30
9	54
12	72
15	90

_____

3.

Input	Output
19	9
54	44
78	68
24	14

_____

Representations Write a rule with a variable for

4. Exercise 1. _____

5. Exercise 2. _____

6. Find a rule for the table. Write the rule in words.

Roses	Cost
12	$24
24	$48
36	$72

_____

_____

7. How much would 72 roses cost?

_____

Test Prep

8. Which is the rule with a variable for the table?

Input	Output
3	81
5	135
7	189
9	243

A. Add 78; $n + 78$

B. Multiply by 17; $17n$

C. Multiply by 27; $27n$

D. Add 86; $n + 86$

9. Writing in Math Explain how you find a rule from a table.

_____

_____

Name_____

Solving Equations

Solve each equation by using mental math.

1. $a + 3 = 35$ _____

2. $1 + e = 21$ _____

3. $3.18n = 31.8$ _____

4. $\frac{45}{p} = 5$ _____

5. $7m = 56$ _____

6. $17x = 51$ _____

Solve each equation by testing the given values for a variable.

7. $y - 9 = 11$

$y = 18, 19,$ or 20 _____

8. $25k = 50$

$k = 1, 2,$ or 3 _____

9. $\frac{z}{4} = 12$

$z = 48, 49,$ or 50 _____

10. $29 - p = 13$

$p = 14, 15,$ or 16 _____

11. Reasoning Write an equation that has a solution of $x = 4.3$.

_____

_____

Test Prep

12. Which is the written equation represented by the picture at the right?

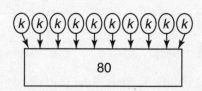

A. $10k = 80$ **B.** $5k = 80$ **C.** $k = 80$ **D.** $2k = 80$

13. Writing in Math Write a description of how mental math can be used to solve the equation $7 = x - 3$.

_____

_____

_____

PROBLEM-SOLVING APPLICATION

Fast Flights

How Fast Do Birds Fly?

Bird	Speed (miles per hour)
Peregrine falcon	168
Hummingbird	71
Mallard	40.6
Wandering albatross	33.6

1. How fast would a hummingbird be flying
   if it doubled its maximum speed?   _____

2. If a wandering albatross doubled its maximum speed,
   could it fly as fast as a hummingbird?

   _____

   _____

   _____

3. **Estimation** Which bird flies about four
   times as fast as a mallard?   _____

4. How fast would a wandering albatross
   be flying if its maximum speed was
   multiplied by 1.8?   _____

5. A mallard is flying at a speed of
   2.8 mph. If it then flies 1.2 times faster,
   how fast is it flying?   _____

6. A certain bird can fly twice as fast as
   a hummingbird. Write an equation
   to express this.   _____

Name_____

The Meaning of Division

Draw a picture or use objects to show each division situation.
Then find the quotient.

1. How many groups of 6 can be formed if there are
   36 students in the class?

2. In a theater with 108 seats, there are 12 times as
   many seats as there are rows. How many rows
   does the theater hold?

3. Ann and Bill need to arrange 36 coins from their
   collection on a page. If they use 4 rows, how many
   coins will be in each row?

Name the operation needed to solve each problem. Then solve.

4. At the airport, 72 people are waiting to board 9 different
   planes. If an equal number of people board each plane,
   how many people get on each plane?

   _____

5. At the halftime show during a football game, a band with
   7 people in 8 rows marches out onto the field to entertain
   the crowd. How many people are in the band?

   _____

Test Prep

6. A high school volleyball team has 20 members. If there is
   an equal number of members from each of the 4 grades,
   how many students from each grade are on the team?

   A. 3   **B.** 4   **C.** 5   **D.** 6

7. **Writing in Math** If there are 50 students in
   the fifth grade and the entire grade had to
   take the same language class, which
   language would have 10 different classes?
   Explain.

   _____

Language	Class Size
French	7
Italian	6
Russian	5
Spanish	10
German	6

Division Patterns

Find each quotient. Use mental math.

1. $27 \div 9 =$ _____   **2.** $270 \div 9 =$ _____   **3.** $2,700 \div 9 =$ _____

4. $24 \div 4 =$ _____   **5.** $240 \div 4 =$ _____   **6.** $2,400 \div 4 =$ _____

7. $720 \div 9 =$ _____   **8.** $140 \div 7 =$ _____   **9.** $2,100 \div 3 =$ _____

10. If a bike race covers 120 mi over 6 days and the cyclists ride the same distance each day, how many miles does each cyclist ride each day?   _____

Use mental math to answer the following questions.

11. If the vehicles are divided evenly between the sections, how many vehicles are in each section?

Dealership Vehicle Storage
Sections of vehicles 4
Vehicles for sale 1,200
Rows per section 10

_____

12. If the vehicles are divided evenly between the rows in each section, how many vehicles are in each row?   _____

13. **Algebra** If $160,000 \div n = 4$, find n.   _____

Test Prep

14. Find $32,000 \div 8$ mentally.

A. 4,000   **B.** 400   **C.** 40   **D.** 4

15. **Writing in Math** Solve the equation $n \times 50 = 5,000$. Explain your solution.

_____

_____

_____

Estimating Quotients

Estimate each quotient. Tell which method you used.

1. 195 ÷ 4 _____ _____

2. 283 ÷ 5 _____ _____

3. 766 ÷ 8 _____ _____

4. 179 ÷ 2 _____ _____

5. $395.20 ÷ 5 _____ _____

6. $31.75 ÷ 8 _____ _____

7. $247.80 ÷ 5 _____ _____

8. **Reasoning** If you use $63.00 ÷ 9 to estimate $62.59 ÷ 9, is $7.00 greater than or less than the exact answer? Explain.

_____

_____

9. A band playing a 3-night concert earned $321.00. Estimate how much the band earned each night.

_____

10. At a department store, a woman's total was $284.00 for 7 items. Estimate the cost of each item.

_____

Test Prep

11. Which is the closest estimate for 213 ÷ 4?

A. 50   **B.** 40   **C.** 30   **D.** 20

12. **Writing in Math** Explain how to estimate 524 ÷ 9.

_____

_____

Name_____

Look for a Pattern

Look for a pattern. Write the missing numbers, or draw the missing figures.

1. 20, 35, 50, _____, _____, _____

2. 32, 28, 24, _____, _____, _____

3. 4, 12, 20, _____, _____, _____

4. 56, 49, 42, _____, _____, _____

5.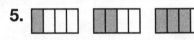

6.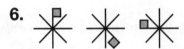

7.
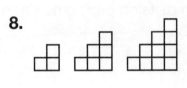

8.

Look for a pattern. Write the missing number sentence.

9. $3 \times 2 = 6$

$3 \times 22 = 66$

$3 \times 222 = 666$

_____

10. $10,000 - 10 = 9,990$

$1,000 - 10 = 990$

$100 - 10 = 90$

_____

11. A banana-nut muffin recipe calls for 3 tbsp of nuts. The recipe makes 4 muffins. For 8 muffins the recipe calls for 6 tbsp of nuts. How many muffins can you make if you use 24 tbsp of nuts?

_____

12. Complete the pattern.

$40.00, $39.00, $37.00, $34.00, _____, _____, _____

Understanding Division

After mowing lawns for one week, John put the money he earned on the table. There were four $100 bills, three $10 bills, and five $1 bills.

1. If John's brother borrowed one of the $100 bills and replaced it with ten $10 bills,

   a. how many $100 bills would there be? _____

   b. how many $10 bills would there be? _____

2. If John needed to divide the money evenly with two other workers, how much would each person receive? _____

3. If John needed to divide the money evenly with four other workers, how much would each person receive? _____

Complete each division problem. You may use play money to help.

4.

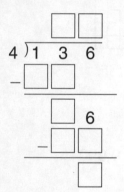

5.

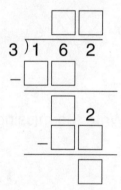

Test Prep

6. If $644.00 is divided equally between 7 people, how much will each person receive?

   A. $82.00   **B.** $92.00   **C.** $93.00   **D.** $103.00

7. Writing in Math Write a story problem using two $100 bills, nine $10 bills, and seven $1 bills.

_____

_____

Name_____

Dividing Whole Numbers

Find each quotient. Check your answers by multiplying.

1. 2)586

2. 3)565

3. 5)718

4. 4)599

5. 5)642

6. 6)354

7. 9)210

8. 8)927

The Paez family lives in Louisville, Kentucky, and has decided to take a road trip for their summer vacation.

9. How many miles will the Paez family drive each day if they decide to take 5 days to drive 865 mi to Dallas?

10. The Paez family decides they want to drive 996 mi to Boston in 6 days. How many miles will they drive each day?

_____

_____

Test Prep

11. If a staff of 9 had to clean a hotel with 198 rooms, how many rooms would each person have to clean if they divided the rooms equally?

A. 29   **B.** 25   **C.** 23   **D.** 22

12. Writing in Math Explain how to check the quotient from a division problem.

_____

_____

_____

Zeros in the Quotient

Find each quotient. Check your answers by multiplying.

1. $490 \div 7 =$ _____

2. $326 \div 3 =$ _____

3. $916 \div 3 =$ _____

4. $720 \div 2 =$ _____

5. $2\overline{)941}$ **6.** $9\overline{)982}$ **7.** $7\overline{)740}$ **8.** $5\overline{)703}$

9. If there are 505 seats in an auditorium divided equally into 5 sections, how many seats are in each section? _____

10. A book company publishes 749 copies of a novel and distributes them to 7 bookstores. If each bookstore were to receive the same amount of novels, how many novels would be sent to each store? _____

Test Prep

11. In one year Dolores and Tom's 4 children saved $420 by recycling cans. When they divided the money equally, how much money did each child receive?

A. $50 **B.** $100 **C.** $105 **D.** $1,500

12. Writing in Math Explain why estimating before you divide $624 \div 6$ helps you place the first digit in the quotient.

_____

_____

_____

Name_____

Dividing Larger Dividends

Find each quotient. Check your answers by multiplying.

1. $6\overline{)3,681}$ **2.** $5\overline{)6,346}$ **3.** $8\overline{)7,258}$ **4.** $6\overline{)2,325}$

5. $4,773 \div 3 =$ _____   **6.** $8,340 \div 9 =$ _____

7. $5,228 \div 7 =$ _____   **8.** $6,574 \div 3 =$ _____

9. Students at Belle School are collecting box tops to get books for their library. Five classes need to collect 7,505 box tops. How many tops must each class collect if the classes collect the same amounts?   _____

10. **Estimation** There are 5 days in a school week. How many school weeks will it take a class from Belle School to collect their tops if it takes them 145 days?   _____

Test Prep

11. 1,504 divided by 4 is

A. equal to 40.   **B.** less than 40.   **C.** less than 400.   **D.** more than 400.

12. **Writing in Math** Predict the number of digits in the quotient for 9,010 divided by 8. Explain.

_____

_____

_____

_____

Dividing Money

Find each quotient. Check your answers by multiplying.

1. $9.03 ÷ 7 = _____

2. $8.24 ÷ 4 = _____

3. $0.75 ÷ 5 = _____

4. $17.55 ÷ 5 = _____

5. 8)$93.76   **6.** 9)$34.65   **7.** 7)$94.15   **8.** 8)$744.48

For 9 and 10, write the dollar amount the farmer received for each pound of potatoes. Then write the year.

9. A farmer received $165.75 for 75 lb of potatoes.

_____ _____

10. A farmer received $402.05 for 473 lb of potatoes.

_____ _____

Average Potato Prices

Year	$ per Pound
1940	0.85
1950	1.50
1960	2.00
1970	2.21
1980	6.55
1990	6.08
2000	4.95

Test Prep

11. Use what you know about patterns and find the missing number. If $25.75 divided by 5 = $5.15, then $257.50 divided by 5 = n.

A. $n = $51.50   **B.** $n = $51.55   **C.** $n = $515.00   **D.** $n = $515.50

12. Writing in Math Explain how dividing $6.75 by 9 is like dividing 675 by 9. How is it different?

_____

_____

Factors and Divisibility

Find all the factors of each number.

1. 36 _____

2. 27 _____

3. 30 _____

4. 75 _____

5. 90 _____

6. 84 _____

Number Sense A number is divisible by 4 if the last two digits are divisible by 4. Write yes on the line if the number is divisible by 4 and no if it is not.

7. 324 _____   **8.** 634 _____   **9.** 172 _____

10. A class of 80 students is graduating from elementary school. The teachers need help figuring out how to line up the students for the ceremony. One row of 80 students would be too long. What other ways could the students be arranged for the ceremony?

_____

_____

11. A number is divisible by another number when the _____ is 0.

Test Prep

12. What factor pair is missing for 45 if you already know 1 and 45, 5 and 9?

A. 7 and 6   **B.** 8 and 6   **C.** 3 and 15   **D.** 4 and 12

13. Writing in Math Explain how to find all the factor pairs of 40.

_____

_____

Prime and Composite Numbers

Write whether each number is prime or composite.

1. 21 _____   **2.** 36 _____   **3.** 31 _____

4. 87 _____   **5.** 62 _____   **6.** 23 _____

Use factor trees to find the prime factorization of each number.

7. 44 _____   **8.** 63 _____

9. 13 _____   **10.** 54 _____

11. Number Sense Audrey says that the prime factorization of 42 is 21 × 2. Is she correct? If not, tell why.

_____

_____

12. Is 4,564,282 prime or composite? Explain how you determined your answer.

_____

_____

Test Prep

13. Which of the following is a prime number?

A. 105   **B.** 27   **C.** 19   **D.** 9

14. Writing in Math Does it matter what two factors you select to complete a factor tree? Explain.

_____

_____

Name_____

Interpreting Remainders

A fifth-grade project was to make something representative of the United States and send it to an address outside the United States. The shipping prices for weight are at the right.

Shipping Prices

Pounds	Price
1–5	$3.00
6–10	$7.00
11–15	$10.00
16–20	$15.00
More than 20	$20.00

1. One group of students pooled their money together before shipping their projects. Four students came up with $24.00. Three out of the 4 packages fell into the same weight category. Which size packages could the students afford to ship?

_____

_____

_____

Another group of students wanted to have the same size boxes for shipping. This group had a total of $30.00.

2. If all 4 students have the same size package, what weight group will their packages fall into?

_____

_____

_____

3. After they have paid for their packages, how much money will be left over? _____

4. If divided equally, how much money will each person get back?

_____

Name_____

Order of Operations

Use the order of operations to evaluate each expression.

1. $4 \times 4 + 3 =$ _____

2. $3 + 6 \times 2 \div 3 =$ _____

3. $24 - (8 \div 2) + 6 =$ _____

4. $(15 - 11) \times (25 \div 5) =$ _____

5. $26 - 4 \times 5 + 2 =$ _____

6. $15 \times (7 - 7) + (5 \times 2) =$ _____

7. $(8 \div 4) \times (7 \times 0) =$ _____

8. $5 \times (6 - 3) + 10 \div (8 - 3) =$ _____

9. Number Sense Which is a true statement,
$5 \times 4 + 1 = 25$ or $3 + 7 \times 2 = 17$? _____

Insert parentheses to make each statement true.

10. $25 \div 5 - 4 = 25$ _____

11. $7 \times 4 - 4 \div 2 = 26$ _____

12. $3 + 5 \times 2 - 10 = 6$ _____

13. Insert parentheses in the expression $6 + 10 \times 2$ so that:

    a. the expression equals 32. _____

    b. the expression equals $(12 + 1) \times 2$. _____

Test Prep

14. Solve $(25 - 7) \times 2 \div 4 + 2$.

    A. 6   **B.** 11   **C.** 5   **D.** 18

15. Writing in Math Write two order of operation problems.
Then trade with a classmate and solve the problems.

_____

_____

44   Use with Lesson 3-13.

Graphing Ordered Pairs

Name the point that is located by each ordered pair.

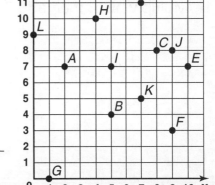

1. (9, 3) _____   **2.** (1, 0) _____

3. (7, 5) _____   **4.** (5, 7) _____

Write the ordered pair for each point.

5. D _____   **6.** C _____

7. E _____   **8.** L _____

Graph each point on the grid to the right.
Label each point.

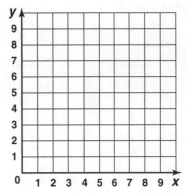

9. M(3, 4)   **10.** Z(6, 5)

11. T(0, 9)   **12.** X(4, 4)

13. P(3, 0)   **14.** A(2, 8)

15. H(7, 7)   **16.** B(2, 9)

17. J(3, 7)   **18.** L(1, 6)

Test Prep

19. Which is the ordered pair for a point 7 units to the right of
the y-axis and 8 units above the x-axis?

A. (8,7)   **B.** (7,8)   **C.** (1,7)   **D.** (1,8)

20. Writing in Math Why are (4, 6) and (6, 4) not at the same
point on a grid?

_____

_____

_____

Name_____

Rules, Tables, and Graphs

Create a table of values for each rule. Use at least four values for *x*.

1. Multiply by 3, then add 2: $3x + 2$ 2. Divide by 3, then add 1: $x \div 3 + 1$

On separate grids, make a graph for each table in Exercises 1 and 2.

3.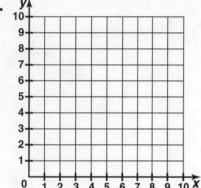

4.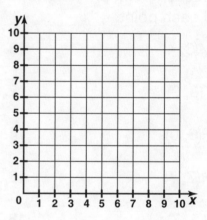

Test Prep

5. Which of the following coordinates does not belong in the
   table of values for the rule: Multiply by 2, then add 1: $2x + 1$.

   A. (2, 5)   **B.** (3, 6)   **C.** (4, 9)   **D.** (0, 1)

6. **Writing in Math** Make a table of values
   for the following rule: Multiply by 3, then
   subtract 2. Explain.

   _____

   _____

   _____

46 Use with Lesson 3-15.

Name_____

Hit Parade

Motown Records is one of the most famous African American owned music companies. During the 1960s and 1970s, Motown artists wrote, recorded, and produced a large number of No. 1 rhythm-and-blues songs and records.

Smokey Robinson was one of Motown's most famous songwriters, singers, producers, and musicians.

1. If Smokey Robinson wrote a total of 176 songs in an 8-year period, how many songs did he write per year?

_____

2. **Writing in Math** Smokey Robinson wrote about 24 No. 1 hits for Motown artists. Explain how you know that the numbers 3 and 4 are both factors of 24.

_____

_____

_____

3. If you paid $53.94 for 6 Smokey Robinson CDs, how much did you pay for each CD?   _____

Stevie Wonder is another famous original Motown songwriter and recording artist.

4. Nine of Stevie Wonder's CDs have a total of 107 songs. About how many songs are on each CD?

_____

5. Robbie bought 7 Stevie Wonder CDs. 4 CDs cost $8.00 each. 2 CDs cost $9.00 each. 1 CD costs $7.00. He gave the cashier $70.00. To calculate his change, Robbie correctly wrote the following equation: Change = $70 - 4 \times 8 - (2 \times 9 + 7)$. How much change did he get?   _____

Dividing by Multiples of 10

Find each quotient. Use mental math.

1. $480 \div 60 =$ _____

2. $8,100 \div 90 =$ _____

3. $32,000 \div 40 =$ _____

4. $15,000 \div 30 =$ _____

5. $4,900 \div 70 =$ _____

6. $16,000 \div 40 =$ _____

Solve for n.

7. $n \div 20 = 60$

8. $n + (400 \div 20) = 27$

9. $420 \div n = 70$

_____ _____ _____

The vegetable farm is planning the summer harvest layout.

10. How many plants will be harvested from each section?

_____

Vegetable Farm Layout
Plants harvested: 60,000
Sections: 20
Rows in each section: 30

11. How many plants will grow in each row?

_____

Test Prep

12. Using the data above, determine how many plants would be harvested in each row if 30,000 plants were harvested and only 10 sections were used.

A. 10   **B.** 100   **C.** 1,000   **D.** 10,000

13. **Writing in Math** Explain the steps you took to figure out your answer for Exercise 12.

_____

_____

_____

Name_____

Estimating with Two-Digit Divisors

Estimate each quotient. Tell which method you used.

1. 269 ÷ 33   _____

2. 158 ÷ 52   _____

3. $910 ÷ 85   _____

4. $250 ÷ 48   _____

5. 200 ÷ 29   _____

6. 1,950 ÷ 94   _____

The Town Traveling Club has 19 members. Estimate each
member's share of each trip expense.

7. transportation $195   **8.** jet ski rentals $635

_____   _____

9. food $385   **10.** Estimate the total expense for
each member of the Town
Traveling Club.

_____

                                              _____

Test Prep

11. Which is a reasonable estimate for 378 ÷ 87?

    A. 1   **B.** 3   **C.** 4   **D.** 7

12. **Writing in Math** Which quotient is greater? Explain how
you know without finding the answer.

    $37.68 ÷ 15 or $35.25 ÷ 15

_____

_____

PROBLEM-SOLVING STRATEGY

Try, Check, and Revise

Solve. Write your answer in a sentence.

1. Bryan needs to build a fence around his rectangular vegetable garden. The length will be 2 ft longer than the width. If he uses 16 ft of fencing, what will be the length and width?

_____

2. Bryan plans on building a larger garden next year. He would like to keep the length the same but extend the width of his garden so that it is square. If Bryan extends the width to make a square, how much fencing will he need to surround the garden?

_____

3. The school district has 294 basketballs to distribute to 36 different teams in the intramural basketball league. If the basketballs are equally distributed, how many basketballs can each team have for practice? How many basketballs will be remaining?

_____

_____

4. Hannah is 8 in. taller than her brother Quinn. If Quinn stood on Hannah's shoulders they would be 80 in. tall. How tall is Quinn?

_____

5. The area of a rectangle is 50 ft. The length is two times the width. What are the length and the width? (Hint: The area of a rectangle is $l \times w$.)

_____

_____

Dividing Whole Numbers by Two-Digits P 4-4

Complete. Find each missing remainder or quotient.

1.
$$37\overline{)120} \quad 3\,R\,\square$$

2.
$$39\overline{)342} \quad \square\,R30$$

3.
$$14\overline{)413} \quad 29\,R\,\square$$

Find each quotient. Check by multiplying.

4. $25\overline{)768}$ **5.** $34\overline{)264}$ **6.** $19\overline{)401}$ **7.** $62\overline{)338}$

8. $599 \div 37 =$ _____

9. $9{,}227 \div 83 =$ _____

10. The school student council sponsored a Switch Day where students were able to switch classes every 20 min. The students are in school for 7 hr. If each student switched the same number of times, how many times did each student get to visit another classroom? (Hint: There are 60 min in 1 hr.)

_____

11. 456 students participated in Switch Day. The students raised money for a charity so that the principal would approve of the day. If the total amount of money raised was $912 and each student brought in the same amount of money, how much did each student raise?

_____

Test Prep

12. Which is $458 \div 73$?

A. 5 R19 **B.** 5 R20 **C.** 6 R19 **D.** 6 R20

13. Writing in Math If you have a two-digit divisor and a three-digit dividend, does the quotient always have the same number of digits? Explain.

_____

_____

Dividing Larger Numbers

Find each quotient. Check your answers by multiplying.

1. $53\overline{)6{,}324}$ **2.** $52\overline{)6{,}348}$ **3.** $86\overline{)31{,}309}$ **4.** $33\overline{)3{,}455}$

5. $17{,}496 \div 91 =$ _____   **6.** $25{,}214 \div 47 =$ _____

7. $2{,}312 \div 26 =$ _____   **8.** $4{,}895 \div 83 =$ _____

The Humphrey family decided to fly from San Francisco, California, to Tokyo, Japan. There were 3 stops along the way.

9. It took the Humphrey family 6 hr to travel from San Francisco to New York. How many kilometers did they travel per hour?

Distances by Plane	
San Francisco to New York	4,140 km
New York to Rome	6,907 km
Rome to New Delhi	5,929 km
New Delhi to Tokyo	5,857 km

_____

10. During the flight from New Delhi to Tokyo, the children played some games. If they switched games every 575 km, how many games did they play?

_____

Test Prep

11. Use the data from Exercises 9–10. When the family arrived in New Delhi from Rome, the youngest son asked the pilot how fast he was flying the plane. The pilot told him about 847 km per hour. How many hours did it take the family to fly from Rome to New Delhi?

A. 5 hr   **B.** 6 hr   **C.** 7 hr   **D.** 8 hr

12. Writing in Math Write a word problem that would require you to use $5{,}621 \div 23$.

_____

Dividing: Choose a Computation Method

Divide and check. Tell which computation method you used.

1. $40\overline{)24{,}000}$ **2.** $40\overline{)6{,}440}$ **3.** $22\overline{)4{,}818}$ **4.** $46\overline{)9{,}936}$

5. $37{,}800 \div 90 =$ _____   **6.** $18{,}000 \div 30 =$ _____

7. $24{,}000 \div 60 =$ _____   **8.** $350{,}000 \div 35 =$ _____

The summer-sale paper was delivered to everyone in the neighborhood.

9. Toni and Bill saw the sale paper and thought they could share the cost of the speed boat with their 4 brothers and sisters. If they divide the cost equally, how much will each person pay?

Speed boat $18,000
Pontoon boat $9,672
Jet ski $2,100

_____

Test Prep

10. Use the data from Exercise 9. Four different families decided to share the cost of the pontoon boat. There would be a total of 8 people sharing the cost of the boat. How much did each person have to pay?

A. $2,418.00   **B.** $1,209.00   **C.** $806.00   **D.** $604.50

11. Writing in Math Describe when it is helpful to use a calculator in dividing. When is it better to use another method?

_____

_____

_____

Name_____

Dividing with Zeros in the Quotient

P 4-7

Find each quotient. Check your answers by multiplying.

1. $60\overline{)6,360}$ **2.** $84\overline{)8,750}$ **3.** $14\overline{)9,828}$ **4.** $57\overline{)36,485}$

5. $12,925 \div 19 =$ _____ **6.** $22,348 \div 37 =$ _____

7. $9,523 \div 28 =$ _____ **8.** $16,451 \div 81 =$ _____

9. If 75 players hit 7,950 baseballs at the batting
cages, how many hits were there for each player? _____

Find each quotient.

10. $3,030 \div 30 =$ _____ **11.** $4,242 \div 42$ _____ **12.** $5,050 \div 50 =$ _____

13. Number Sense Explain the reason for the pattern in the
quotients in Exercises 10–12.

_____

_____

Test Prep

14. Which is $17,889 \div 88$?

A. 203 **B.** 203 R25 **C.** 204 R1 **D.** 205

15. Writing in Math Write a problem with a two-digit divisor, a five-
digit dividend, and a quotient of 308. Explain how you did it.

_____

_____

_____

54 Use with Lesson 4-7.

Name_____

Multiple-Step Problems

Write and answer the hidden question or
questions in each problem and then solve the
problem. Write your answer in a complete sentence.

Storewide Sale	
Jeans	$29.95 for 1 pair OR 2 pairs for $55.00
T-shirts	$9.95 for 1 OR 3 T-shirts for $25.00

1. Sue bought 2 pairs of jeans and a belt
   that cost $6.95. The tax on the items
   was $5.85. Sue paid the cashier $70.00.
   How much money did Sue receive in change?

   _____

   _____

2. A recreation department purchased 12 T-shirts for day
   camp. The department does not have to pay sales tax. It
   paid with a $100.00 bill. How much change did it receive?

   _____

   _____

   _____

3. When Mrs. Johnson saw the sale, she decided to get
   clothes for each child in her family. She bought each of her
   6 children a pair of jeans and a T-shirt. She paid $14.35 in
   sales tax. How much was Mrs. Johnson's total bill?

   _____

   _____

   _____

4. **Writing in Math** Write a two-step problem about buying something
   at the mall that has a hidden question. Tell what the hidden
   question is and solve your problem. Use $8.95 somewhere in
   your equation. Write your answer in a complete sentence.

   _____

Dividing Decimals by 10, 100, and 1,000

Find each quotient. Use mental math.

1. $86.6 \div 10 =$ _____

2. $192.5 \div 100 =$ _____

3. $1.99 \div 100 =$ _____

4. $0.87 \div 10 =$ _____

5. $228.55 \div 1,000 =$ _____

6. $0.834 \div 100 =$ _____

7. $943.35 \div 1,000 =$ _____

8. $1.25 \div 10 =$ _____

Algebra Write 10, 100, or 1,000 for each n.

9. $78.34 \div n = 0.7834$ **10.** $0.32 \div n = 0.032$ **11.** $(75.34 - 25.34) \div n = 5$

_____   _____   _____

12. There are 145 children taking swimming lessons at the pool. If 10 children will be assigned to each instructor, how many instructors need to be hired?

_____

13. The instructors must pass a test before getting the job. The instructors must swim 2 mi. If it takes Jane 5 min every half mile, how long should it take her to finish?

_____

Test Prep

14. Ronald ran 534.3 mi in 100 days. If he ran an equal distance each day, how many miles did he run per day?

A. 5   **B.** 5.13   **C.** 5.343   **D.** 6.201

15. Writing in Math Carlos says that $17.43 \div 100$ is the same as 174.3×0.01. Is he correct? Explain.

_____

_____

Name_____

Dividing Money by Two-Digit Divisors

Find each quotient. Check your answers by multiplying. (Round to the nearest cent, if necessary.)

1. $11\overline{)\$8.91}$ **2.** $61\overline{)\$43.92}$ **3.** $12\overline{)\$84.24}$ **4.** $28\overline{)\$4.20}$

5. $\$87.08 \div 82 =$ _____   **6.** $\$93.49 \div 59 =$ _____

7. $\$17.83 \div 5 =$ _____   **8.** $\$114.38 \div 19 =$ _____

Number Sense Decide if each quotient is greater than or less than $1.00.

9. $\$76.65 \div 73$ _____

10. $\$9.30 \div 62$ _____

11. Estimation Is the quotient you get when you divide $550.81 by 70 closer to $0.80, $8.00, or $80.00?   _____

Test Prep

12. If 6 people split a dinner bill of $180.30, how much will each person pay?

    A. $30.05   **B.** $30.15   **C.** $30.50   **D.** $30.55

13. Writing in Math Explain why $46.50 ÷ 30 could not be $15.00.

_____

_____

_____

_____

Name_____

Dividing Decimals by Whole Numbers

Find each quotient. Check by multiplying.

1. $13\overline{)68.9}$ 2. $35\overline{)412.3}$ 3. $90\overline{)14.4}$ 4. $60\overline{)53.4}$

5. $123.08 \div 34 =$ _____   6. $0.57 \div 30 =$ _____

7. $562.86 \div 59 =$ _____   8. $24.4 \div 80 =$ _____

9. If a package of granola bars with 12 bars costs
   $3.48, how much does each granola bar cost?   _____

10. John paid $7.99 for 3 boxes of cereal. The tax
    was $1.69. Excluding tax, how much did John
    pay for each box of cereal if they all were the
    same price?   _____

Test Prep

11. $64.82 \div 11$ is

    A. a little more than 6.   B. a little less than 6.

    C. a little more than 60.   D. a little less than 60.

12. **Writing in Math** Explain how to divide 0.12 by 8.

    _____

    _____

    _____

    _____

Name_____

Listen to This

The Federal Communications Commission (FCC) reported that there were 12,615 radio stations in the United States in 1999.

1. The FCC reported that there were 4,783 AM radio stations in the United States in 1999. Round 4,783 to the nearest hundred.

_____

2. Use that number to determine the average number of AM radio stations per state in the United States. (Hint: There are 50 states in the United States.)

_____

_____

3. There were 5,766 FM radio stations in the United States in 1999. Find the average number of FM radio stations per state in the United States. Round your answer to the nearest one.

_____

_____

4. In a 30-year period between 1970 and 2000, 6,108 new radio stations were started in the United States. If the number of radio stations started was the same each year, about how many radio stations were started per year?

_____

_____

5. During a 20 hr broadcast day, the average United States radio station broadcasts about 280 min of commercials. About how many minutes of commercials are broadcast each hour? (Remember: There are 60 min in 1 hr.)

_____

Collecting Data from a Survey

Identify each statement as either a fact or an opinion.

1. Dogs are the best pets to own. _____

2. Nine students received As on their tests. _____

3. Five students live 3 blocks from school. _____

4. Three people is a good number for a team. _____

5. Spaghetti is the tastiest meal. _____

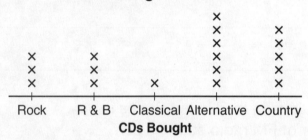

Music Bought in Class B

Rock   R & B   Classical Alternative Country

CDs Bought

6. If the entire class responded to the survey, how
   many students are in the class? _____

7. What information was collected about music?

_____

Test Prep

8. Use the line plot above. Which type of CDs did students buy most often?

    A. Alternative   **B.** Classical   **C.** Country   **D.** Rock

9. **Writing in Math** Write a survey question that might gather
   the following information.

   In one school there are 6 sets of twins, 2 sets of triplets,
   and 1 set of quadruplets.

_____

_____

Bar Graphs

The data at the right shows the number of students who bought lunch the first week of school during the 1999–2000 and 2000–2001 school years. The data has been rounded to the nearest ten.

Students Buying Lunch

Days	1999–2000	2000–2001
Mon.	90	140
Tue.	60	70
Wed.	120	160
Thur.	130	140
Fri.	100	120

1. Which data would have the shortest bar on a graph?

_____

2. Complete the graph to the right.

3. During which school year did the most students buy lunches? How many more?

_____

_____

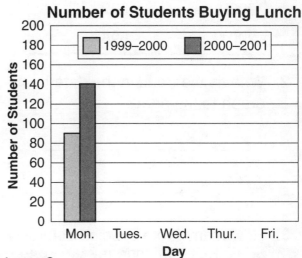

4. Overall, what pattern do you see occurring from the 1999–2000 school year to the 2000–2001 school year?

_____

Test Prep

5. Use the graph above. On which day of the week was an average of 100 lunches sold?

   A. Tuesday   **B.** Wednesday   **C.** Thursday   **D.** Friday

6. **Writing in Math** Is a data file needed to make a bar graph? Explain.

_____

_____

Line Graphs

1. Make a line graph of the data. Use a scale from 550 to 600 and an interval of 5 for the number of species.

Endangered U.S. Plants

Year	Number of Species
1997	553
1998	567
1999	581
2000	592
2001	595

2. What is the trend in the data in the graph to the right?

_____

_____

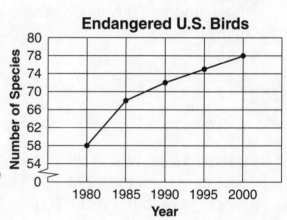

Endangered U.S. Birds

3. How many more species of birds were endangered in 2000 than in 1980?

_____

Test Prep

4. Which is the trend if the line on a graph is rising from left to right?

   A. Staying the same   **B.** Increasing

   C. Decreasing   **D.** Doubling

5. **Writing in Math** The numbers in a data file are 71, 56, 62, 77, and 38. What scale would you use to graph the data? Explain your choice.

_____

_____

Stem-and-Leaf Plots

The data file below shows the ages of
people in a movie theater.

> **Ages of People at the Movie Theater**
> 25, 16, 42, 34, 65, 54, 10, 18, 45, 34,
> 23, 33, 51, 36, 21, 19, 18, 34, 15, 50

1. Make a stem-and-leaf plot of the data.
   Title the plot "Ages of People at the
   Movie Theater."

2. What is the range of the data? How do you know?

   _____

   _____

3. How many people over 20 years old
   watched the movie?   _____

4. How many people under 20 years old
   watched the movie?   _____

5. What age was most frequent at this
   movie theater?   _____

Test Prep

6. Which age group had the most people at the movie?

   A. People under twenty   **B.** People in their twenties

   C. People in their thirties   **D.** People in their forties

7. **Writing in Math** Is Bill's explanation
   correct? If not, tell why.

   _____

   _____

   _____

> Bill's Explanation
>
> How do you make a
> stem-and-leaf plot?
>
> First, you list all the first digits
> on the left in the plot.
>
> Then you list all the second digits
> on the right in the plot.

Name_____

Make a Graph

Zoos in the United States have different budgets. The table shows budgets for five U.S. zoos in 2001. The budgets are in millions of dollars.

1. Make a bar graph using the data to the right.

Budgets of U.S. Zoos in 2001

Zoo Budget	
Albuquerque Biological Park	$9
Cleveland Metroparks Zoo	$12
Oregon Zoo	$15
Phoenix Zoo	$16
San Diego Zoo	$56

2. Which zoo had the largest budget? The smallest budget?

_____

_____

3. What was the greatest difference between zoo budgets?

_____

_____

Name_____

Mean, Median, and Mode

1. Find the mean of this data set: 225 342 288 552 263   _____

2. Find the median of this data set: 476 234 355 765 470   _____

3. Find the mode of this data set:
   16 7 8 5 16 7 8 4 7 8 16 7   _____

4. Find the range of this data set:
   64 76 46 88 88 43 99 50 55   _____

5. **Reasoning** Would the mode change if a 76 was added to the data in Exercise 4?

   _____

   _____

The table gives the math test scores for Mrs. Jung's fifth-grade class.

76	54	92	88	76	88
75	93	92	68	88	76
76	88	80	70	88	72
Test Scores					

6. Find the mean of the data.   _____

7. Find the mode of the data.   _____

8. Find the median of the data.   _____

9. What is the range of the data set?   _____

Test Prep

10. Find the mean of this data set: 247, 366, 785, 998.

    A. 599   **B.** 598   **C.** 589   **D.** 579

11. **Writing in Math** Will a set of data always have a mode?
    Explain your answer.

    _____

    _____

Name_____

Circle Graphs

Three thousand fifth graders were asked which foreign continent they would most like to visit. The results are shown in the circle graph.

Continent to Visit

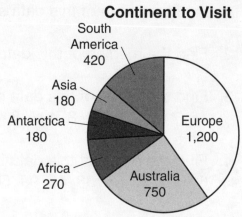

1. Which continent was most popular?

   _____

2. How many students were most interested in Africa?

   _____

3. **Estimation** About how many more students wanted to go to Europe than to Australia?

   _____

Favorite Sports

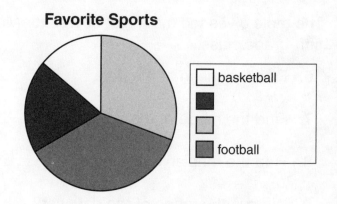

4. Bill surveyed the 100 students in fifth grade. Complete the graph to the right by labeling the missing categories. More students liked baseball than soccer.

Test Prep

5. 40 people were asked to name their favorite meal. 5 said breakfast, 10 said lunch, 5 said snack, and 20 said dinner. Which meal selection will section 2 represent?

   Favorite Meals

   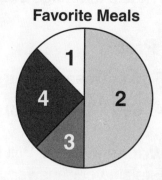

   A. Breakfast   **B.** Lunch

   C. Snack   **D.** Dinner

6. **Writing in Math** Explain how you would know which sections of the graph would represent the other meal situations.

   _____

   _____

Choosing an Appropriate Graph

Tell what type of graph would be most appropriate to represent the data listed.

1. Flower sales over a week _____

_____

2. Where the total amount of income for one month is spent

_____

3. Describe the trend in attendance at the pool for the week of June 3.

_____

_____

_____

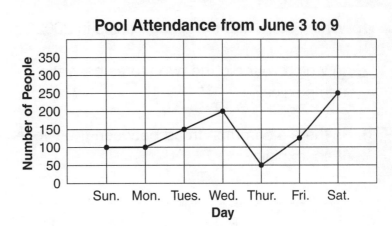

Pool Attendance from June 3 to 9

4. Predict what may have been the cause for the decline on Thursday.

_____

Test Prep

5. Use the graph above. What day did the pool's attendance peak?

A. Thursday   **B.** Saturday   **C.** Wednesday   **D.** Sunday

6. Writing in Math When should you use a double bar graph or double line graph?

_____

_____

_____

PROBLEM-SOLVING SKILL   **P 5-9**
Writing to Compare

Analyze the graphs below. Then answer the questions.

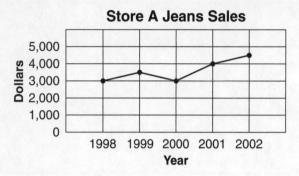

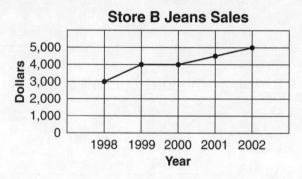

1. Which store had the greater sales in 2002?   _____

2. In which year did the two stores have the
   same sales?   _____

3. Is there a common trend between the two jeans stores?
   If so, explain.

   _____

   _____

   _____

4. Which graph shows a slow increase over time?   _____

5. If the stores continue the trends that are represented in the
   graph, which store do you think will have higher sales in
   5 years? Explain your answer.

   _____

   _____

   _____

6. Which store has a greater range in sales?
   What is the range?   _____

Name_____

Predicting Outcomes

The nature club is planning a field trip. They have decided to write their destination choices on slips of paper and have their instructor select the destination by drawing a slip of paper out of a bag. The slips of paper shown below are the destination choices in the bag.

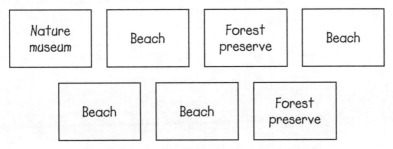

| Nature museum | Beach | Forest preserve | Beach |

| Beach | Beach | Forest preserve |

1. Is it equally likely that the instructor will draw the nature museum or the forest preserve? Explain. _____

   _____

   _____

2. Which destination is the instructor least likely to draw? _____

3. Which destination is the instructor most likely to draw? _____

Test Prep

4. Use data from Exercises 1–3. What is the chance of the instructor drawing the nature museum?

   A. 3 out of 7   **B.** 2 out of 7

   C. 1 out of 7   **D.** Impossible event

5. **Writing in Math** Explain the difference between an outcome and a favorable outcome.

   _____

   _____

Listing Outcomes

The coach is trying to decide in what order Jane, Pete, and Lou
will run a relay race.

1. Complete the tree diagram below to show the sample space.

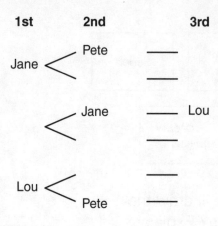

| 1st | 2nd | 3rd |

2. How many possible outcomes are there in
   the sample space?   _____

3. After the first runner is chosen, how many
   choices are there for the second runner?   _____

Test Prep

4. Tom, Bill, John, and Ed are running for school president.
   The person in second place automatically becomes
   vice-president. How many possible outcomes are there
   in the sample space?

   A. 6   **B.** 9   **C.** 10   **D.** 12

5. **Writing in Math** Why are Tom, Bill, John, and Ed equally
   likely to win school president? Explain.

   _____

   _____

   _____

Name_____

Expressing Probability as a Fraction

Tom put 4 yellow marbles, 2 blue marbles, 6 red marbles,
and 5 black marbles in a bag.

1. Find the P(yellow).   _____

2. Find the P(blue).   _____

3. Find the P(red).   _____

4. Find the P(black).   _____

A bag contains 12 slips of paper of the same size. Each slip has
one number on it, 1–12.

5. Find the P(even number).   _____

6. Find the P(a number less than 6).   _____

7. Find the P(an odd number).   _____

8. Find the P(a number greater than 8).   _____

9. Describe an impossible event.

_____

Test Prep

10. A cube has 6 sides and is numbered 1 through 6. If the cube
is tossed, what is the probability that a 3 will be tossed?

A. $\frac{1}{6}$ **B.** $\frac{2}{6}$ **C.** $\frac{3}{6}$ **D.** $\frac{6}{6}$

11. Explain the probability of tossing a prime number when you
toss the cube with numbers 1 through 6.

_____

_____

Name_____

School Uniforms

School uniforms are becoming more popular at grade schools in the United States. A Kids USA Survey asked about 1,600 girls and 1,300 boys what their favorite colors were.

Favorite Uniform Colors for Girls (per 100 surveyed)

Color	Number of Girls
Blue	24
White	8
Red	7
Green	12
Yellow	3
Black	30
Other	16

1. Which color got the most votes? _____

   The least? _____

2. Which two colors were the closest in votes?

   _____

3. Complete the bar graph for the data.

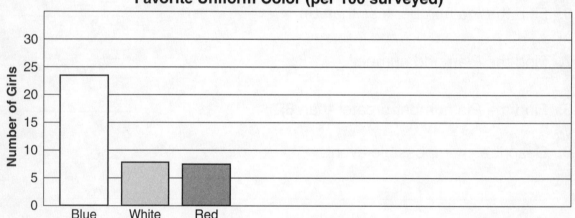

Favorite Uniform Color (per 100 surveyed)

4. Write the number of boys numbers for each color in increasing order.

   _____

   _____

5. What is the median? _____

6. What is the mode? _____

Favorite Uniform Colors for Boys (per 100 surveyed)

Color	Number of Boys
Blue	22
White	7
Red	7
Green	13
Yellow	3
Black	31
Other	17

Geometric Ideas

Use the diagram at the right. Name the following.

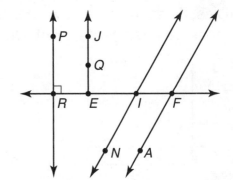

1. three points

_____

2. a ray

_____

3. two intersecting lines but not perpendicular

_____

4. two parallel lines   _____

5. a line segment   _____

6. two perpendicular lines   _____

7. Reasoning Can a line segment have two midpoints? Explain.

_____

_____

_____

Test Prep

8. Which type of lines are shown by the figure?

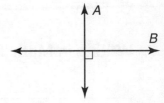

A. Intersecting   **B.** Parallel

C. Perpendicular   **D.** Curved

9. Writing in Math Draw and label two perpendicular line segments $\overline{KL}$ and $\overline{MN}$.

Measuring and Classifying Angles

Classify each angle as *acute, right, obtuse,* or *straight.* Then
measure each angle. (Hint: Draw longer sides if necessary.)

1.

2.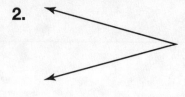

_____   _____

Draw an angle with each measure.

3. 120°   4. 180°

5. Draw an acute angle. Label it with the letters
   A, B, and *C.* What is the measure of the angle?   _____

Test Prep

6. Which kind of angle is shown in the figure below?

   A. Acute   **B.** Obtuse

   C. Right   **D.** Straight

7. **Writing in Math** Explain how to use a protractor to measure an angle.

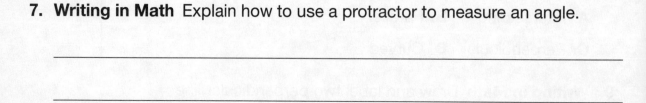

_____

_____

_____

Name_____

Classifying Triangles

Classify each triangle by its sides and then by its angles.

1.

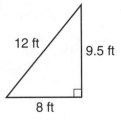

2.

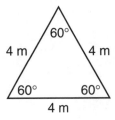

_____   _____

_____   _____

The measures of two angles of a triangle are given. Find the measure of the third angle.

3. 47°, 62°, _____   **4.** 29°, 90°, _____

5. 75°, 75°, _____   **6.** 54°, 36°, _____

7. Judy bought a new tent for a camping trip. Look at the side of the tent with the opening to classify the triangle by its sides and its angles.

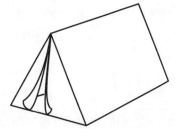

Test Prep

8. Which describes a scalene triangle?

A. 4 equal sides   **B.** 3 equal sides   **C.** 2 equal sides   **D.** 0 equal sides

9. Writing in Math The lengths of two sides of a triangle are 15 in. each. The third side measures 10 in. What type of triangle is this? Explain your answer using geometric terms.

_____

_____

Name _____

Classifying Quadrilaterals

Classify each quadrilateral. Be as specific as possible.

1.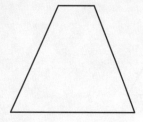

2.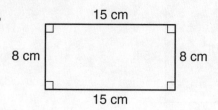

_____

_____

3.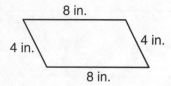

4.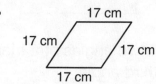

_____

_____

The measures of three angles of a quadrilateral are given. Find the measure of the fourth angle.

5. 90°, 145°, 78°, _____

6. 110°, 54°, 100°, _____

7. Name the vertices of the square.

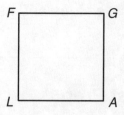

_____

Test Prep

8. Three of the angles of a quadrilateral measure 80°, 100°, and 55°. Which is the measure of the fourth angle?

A. 115°   **B.** 120°   **C.** 125°   **D.** 130°

9. Writing in Math Can a trapezoid have four obtuse angles? Explain.

_____

_____

_____

Name_____

Solve a Simpler Problem

Solve the simpler problems. Use the solutions to
help you solve the original problem.

1. Reggie is designing a triangular magazine rack with
   5 shelves. The top shelf will hold 1 magazine. The
   second shelf will hold 3 magazines, and the third
   shelf will hold 5 magazines. This pattern continues
   to the bottom shelf. How many magazines will the
   magazine rack hold altogether?

   Simpler Problem What is the pattern?

   _____

   _____

   How many magazines will the fourth
   shelf hold?   _____

   How many magazines will the bottom
   shelf hold?   _____

   Solution: _____

   _____

2. At the deli, you receive 1 free sub after you buy 8 subs.
   How many free subs will you receive from the deli if you
   buy 24 subs?

   _____

   _____

3. The chef has 5 different kinds of pasta and 3 different flavors
   of sauce. How many different meals is she able to make?

   _____

   _____

Name_____

Writing to Describe

Solve each problem. You may use a brainstorming table to help plan your description.

1. Use geometric terms to describe three properties of a square.

_____

_____

_____

2. Use mathematical terms to describe the numbers in each set.

_____

_____

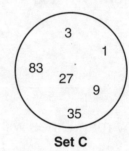

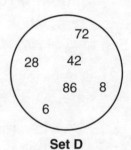

Set C   Set D

3. Mariam created two patterns. Use mathematical terms to describe the numbers in each pattern.

Pattern 1: 12, 16, 20, 24, 28, 32

Pattern 2: 1, 2, 4, 8, 16, 32, 64

_____

_____

4. Use geometric terms to describe three properties of this trapezoid.

_____

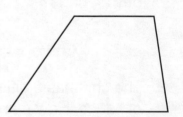

_____

_____

Name_____

Congruence and Similarity

Do the figures in each pair appear to be similar? If so, are they also congruent?

1.

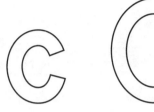

_____

_____

2.

_____

_____

Is each situation an example of congruent or similar figures? Explain your reasoning.

3. When baking bread, the baker uses two sizes of loaf pans. One loaf pan fits inside the other.

_____

_____

4. A friend gave you and five friends each a quarter.

_____

_____

Test Prep

5. If Figure A is similar to Figure B, which is the measure of ∠XYZ in Figure A?

   A. 90°   B. 58°

   C. 45°   D. 32°

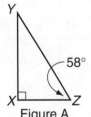

Figure A

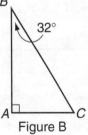

Figure B

6. **Writing in Math** If two circles are congruent, are the diameters the same length? Explain.

_____

_____

Transformations

Tell whether the figures in each pair are related by a flip, slide, or turn. If a turn, describe it.

1.

   _____

2.

   _____

3. On a compass, if you are standing at 0° and you turn to your right to make a 90° turn, what fraction of a turn is that?

   _____

4. If a figure is flipped over the dashed line and then rotated a $\frac{1}{4}$ turn counterclockwise, which of the figures below shows the result?

   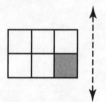

   A.   **B.** 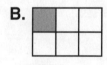 **C.**   **D.**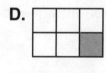

Test Prep

5. Which term describes the mirror image of a figure?

   A. Slide   **B.** Flip   **C.** Turn   **D.** Pattern

6. **Writing in Math** Mark says that the figure above was flipped. Faith says that it made a $\frac{3}{4}$ turn. Steven says that it made a 90° turn. Who is correct?

   _____

Name_____

Symmetry

How many lines of symmetry does each figure have? You may fold your paper to check.

1.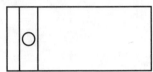

_____

2.

_____

3. Reasoning How many lines of symmetry does an equilateral triangle have? Explain.

_____

_____

Part of a symmetric trademark is shown. Complete each drawing.

4.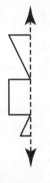

5.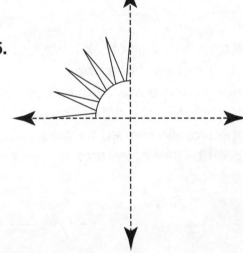

Test Prep

6. Which figure has more than two lines of symmetry?

A.   **B.**    **C.**   **D.**

7. Writing in Math Draw a shape or figure that has more than 2 lines of symmetry. Put the lines of symmetry into your drawing.

Name_____

The Shape We Are In

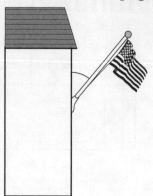

1. Tarah hung an American flag from the front
porch of her house. She placed it in a flag
stand on one of the posts of the porch.
Measure the angle of the flagpole from
the post.

_____

2. Construct a circle. Use the measure of the radius below.

3. Karen and Willie took a walk
on the streets near their
home. The path of their walk
is shown at the right. Classify
the triangle formed by the
path by its angles and
its sides.

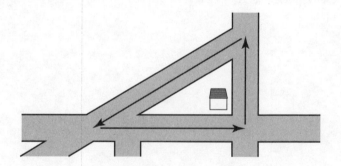

_____

_____

4. Part of a symmetric figure is shown. Complete the drawing.

Meanings of Fractions

Write the fraction that names the shaded part or point
on a number line.

1.  _____

2. 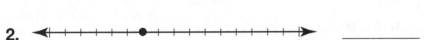 _____

3. 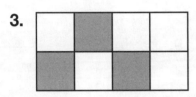 _____

In 4 and 5, draw a model to show each fraction.

4. $\frac{4}{8}$ as part of a set

5. $\frac{5}{10}$ as part of a region

6. Number Sense If $\frac{5}{17}$ of a region is shaded, what
part is not shaded?

_____

7. Camp Big Trees has 3 red canoes and 4 blue
canoes. What fraction of the canoes are red?

_____

Test Prep

8. Which is the value of x, if $\frac{x}{9} = 1$?

A. 0   **B.** 1   **C.** 9   **D.** 19

9. Writing in Math Trisha says that if $\frac{5}{7}$ of her pencils are
yellow, then $\frac{2}{7}$ are not yellow. Is she correct? Explain.

_____

_____

Fractions and Division

Give each answer as a fraction.

1. $3 \div 7$ _____   **2.** $4 \div 9$ _____   **3.** $1 \div 5$ _____

4. $2 \div 11$ _____   **5.** $3 \div 5$ _____   **6.** $5 \div 8$ _____

At a golf course, there are 18 holes. Of the 18 holes, 3 are par threes, 8 are par fours, and 7 are par fives. What fraction of the holes are

7. par fives? _____   **8.** par threes? _____   **9.** par fours? _____

10. Number Sense Explain how you know that $7 \div 9$ is less than 1.

_____

_____

11. After school, Chase spends 20 min reading, 30 min practicing the piano, 15 min cleaning his room, and 40 min doing his homework. Chase is busy for 105 min. What fraction of the time does he spend cleaning his room?   _____

Test Prep

12. Venietta read 4 books in 7 weeks. How many books did she read each week?

A. $\frac{6}{7}$ **B.** $\frac{4}{7}$ **C.** $\frac{3}{7}$ **D.** $\frac{2}{7}$

13. Writing in Math In 5 min, Peter completed 2 math problems. Yvonne says he did $\frac{3}{5}$ of a problem each minute. Is she correct? Explain.

_____

_____

_____

Mixed Numbers

Write an improper fraction and a mixed number for each model.

1. 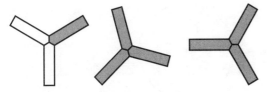 _____

2. 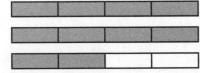 _____

Write each improper fraction as a mixed number.

3. $\frac{12}{7}$ _____   **4.** $\frac{7}{3}$ _____   **5.** $\frac{5}{2}$ _____

6. $\frac{9}{4}$ _____   **7.** $\frac{29}{13}$ _____   **8.** $\frac{34}{8}$ _____

Write each mixed number as an improper fraction.

9. $2\frac{4}{5}$ _____   **10.** $8\frac{7}{9}$ _____   **11.** $3\frac{6}{7}$ _____

12. $7\frac{1}{8}$ _____   **13.** $4\frac{3}{7}$ _____   **14.** $5\frac{1}{4}$ _____

Test Prep

15. Jasmine has 41 lb of dog food to evenly pour into 5 dishes.
How many pounds of dog food should she pour in each dish?

    A. $4\frac{1}{5}$ lb   **B.** $8\frac{1}{5}$ lb   **C.** 10 lb   **D.** $11\frac{1}{8}$ lb

16. **Writing in Math** Hank needs 3 quarters to play one video
game each time. If he has 14 quarters, how many times
can he play? Explain.

_____

_____

_____

_____

Estimating Fractional Amounts

Estimate the shaded part of each.

1. 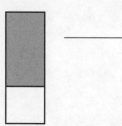 _____

2. 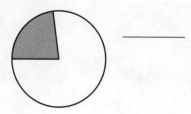 _____

3.  _____

4. Reasoning If about $\frac{2}{3}$ of a piece of cloth is used, about what fraction of the cloth was not used? _____

Estimate the fraction in each region for the most popular sports.

5. basketball _____

6. football _____

7. baseball _____

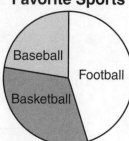

Favorite Sports

Test Prep

8. Jim ate about $\frac{1}{4}$ of the pizza, and Jane ate about $\frac{1}{4}$ of the pizza. About how much of the pizza is left?

A. $\frac{1}{4}$ **B.** $\frac{2}{5}$ **C.** $\frac{2}{8}$ **D.** $\frac{2}{4}$

9. Writing in Math Explain how you know that $\frac{1}{2}$ of a grapefruit is larger than $\frac{1}{2}$ of a grape.

_____

_____

_____

Name_____

Fractions and Mixed Numbers
on the Number Line

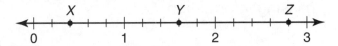

What fraction or mixed number represents each point?

1. Point *X* _____   **2.** Point *Y* _____   **3.** Point *Z* _____

Draw a number line to show each set of numbers. Then order the numbers from least to greatest.

4. $\frac{2}{3}, \frac{5}{6}, \frac{1}{6}$ _____

5. $1\frac{3}{4}, 1\frac{9}{10}, 1\frac{1}{2}$ _____

Test Prep

6. Which number would be to the right of $7\frac{9}{10}$ on a number line?

A. $7\frac{10}{12}$ **B.** $7\frac{7}{8}$ **C.** $7\frac{25}{30}$ **D.** $7\frac{10}{11}$

7. Writing in Math If, on a number line, point *R* is $3\frac{3}{8}$ and point *T* is $3\frac{7}{8}$, where could point *S* be if it is between points *R* and *T*? Explain.

_____

_____

_____

Extra or Missing Information

Decide if each problem has extra or missing information. Solve if you have enough information.

1. Jared and Cody went on a backpacking trip for 3 days. They brought 2 boxes of spaghetti. Each box weighed 16 oz. They also brought 4 cans of sauce. Each can weighed 8 oz. How many ounces did each person carry if each carried the same amount?

_____

2. Each backpack weighed 25 lb and each tent weighed 3 lb. If there are 30 backpackers, how much did their backpacks weigh altogether?

_____

For 3–5, use the table at the right.

3. The backpackers hiked the Black Hawk trail on Monday. They planned to hike on Tuesday. What is the total number of trails they hiked on Monday and Tuesday?

Trail Name	Length
Hiawatha	6 mi
Pontiac	2 mi
Black Hawk	10 mi
Keokuk	7 mi

_____

4. How much longer is twice around the Black Hawk trail than twice around the Hiawatha trail?

_____

5. Mariah hiked the Pontiac trail 5 days in 1 week. She did not hike on Wednesday and Friday. How many miles did she hike throughout 1 week?

_____

Name _____

Understanding Equivalent Fractions

Write two fractions that name each shaded part.

1. 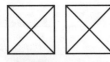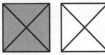 _____

2.  _____

3.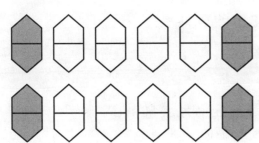

_____

4.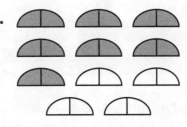

_____

5. Trinity attends 6 classes. Each class lasts 1 hr. Her younger sister attends 10 classes that last 30 min each. Who is in class longer? How much longer?

_____

_____

Test Prep

6. If 2 out of 3 gym balls are blue, how many out of 6 gym balls are blue?

A. 2   **B.** 3   **C.** 4   **D.** 5

7. Writing in Math Explain how you know that $\frac{4}{5} = \frac{8}{10}$.

_____

_____

_____

Name_____

Equivalent Fractions

Name two equivalent fractions for each fraction.

1. $\frac{5}{15}$ _____

2. $\frac{6}{36}$ _____

3. $\frac{2}{12}$ _____

4. $\frac{4}{28}$ _____

5. $\frac{3}{21}$ _____

6. $\frac{2}{11}$ _____

Find the missing number to make the fractions equivalent.

7. $\frac{9}{13} = \frac{18}{x}$ _____

8. $\frac{12}{30} = \frac{n}{90}$ _____

9. $\frac{q}{54} = \frac{2}{9}$ _____

10. $\frac{14}{h} = \frac{7}{20}$ _____

11. Renie gave each of six people $\frac{1}{10}$ of a veggie pizza. Renie has $\frac{2}{5}$ of the pizza left. Explain how this is true.

_____

_____

_____

Test Prep

12. Which fraction is equivalent to $\frac{3}{7}$?

    A. $\frac{3}{6}$ B. $\frac{6}{14}$ C. $\frac{3}{17}$ D. $\frac{7}{7}$

13. **Writing in Math** Jacqueline has four $5 bills. She bought a shirt for $10. She has spent half of her money. Explain how much money Jacqueline spent. Use equivalent fractions.

_____

_____

_____

_____

_____

Greatest Common Factor

Find the GCF of each pair of numbers.

1. 15, 50 _____   **2.** 6, 27 _____   **3.** 10, 25 _____

4. 18, 32 _____   **5.** 7, 28 _____   **6.** 54, 108 _____

7. 25, 55 _____   **8.** 14, 48 _____   **9.** 81, 135 _____

10. Number Sense Can the GCF of 16 and 42 be less than 16? Explain.

_____

_____

_____

11. A restaurant received a shipment of 42 gal of
orange juice and 18 gal of cranberry juice. The
juice needs to be equally poured into containers.
What is the largest amount of juice that each
container can hold of each kind of juice?   _____

12. At a day camp, there are 56 girls and 42 boys.
The campers need to be split into equal groups.
Each has either all girls or all boys. What is the
greatest number of campers each group can have?   _____

Test Prep

13. Which is the GCF of 24 and 64?

   A. 4   **B.** 8   **C.** 14   **D.** 12

14. Writing in Math Do all even numbers have 2 as a factor?
Explain.

_____

_____

_____

Name_____

Fractions in Simplest Form

Write each fraction in simplest form.

1. $\frac{5}{10}$ _____

2. $\frac{6}{24}$ _____

3. $\frac{9}{27}$ _____

4. $\frac{3}{15}$ _____

5. $\frac{10}{12}$ _____

6. $\frac{9}{15}$ _____

7. $\frac{2}{18}$ _____

8. $\frac{25}{60}$ _____

9. $\frac{12}{72}$ _____

10. $\frac{30}{70}$ _____

11. $\frac{22}{48}$ _____

12. $\frac{16}{56}$ _____

13. $\frac{9}{90}$ _____

14. $\frac{72}{81}$ _____

15. $\frac{7}{28}$ _____

16. **Number Sense** Explain how you can tell $\frac{4}{5}$ is in simplest form.

_____

_____

_____

Write in simplest form.

17. What fraction of the problems on the math test will be word problems?

_____

Math Test

⇒ 20 Multiple-choice problems

⇒ 10 Fill in the blanks

⇒ 5 Word problems

18. What fraction of the problems on the math test will be multiple-choice problems?

_____

Test Prep

19. Which is the simplest form of $\frac{10}{82}$?

A. $\frac{1}{8}$ B. $\frac{1}{22}$ C. $\frac{10}{82}$ D. $\frac{5}{41}$

20. **Writing in Math** Explain how you can find the simplest form of $\frac{100}{1,000}$.

_____

_____

94 Use with Lesson 7-10.

Name_____

Write >, <, or = for each ◯. You may use fraction strips or drawings to help.

1. $\frac{4}{12}$ ◯ $\frac{4}{16}$

2. $\frac{7}{14}$ ◯ $\frac{3}{5}$

3. $\frac{5}{10}$ ◯ $\frac{1}{2}$

4. $\frac{1}{9}$ ◯ $\frac{1}{6}$

5. $\frac{2}{6}$ ◯ $\frac{2}{7}$

6. $\frac{3}{9}$ ◯ $\frac{1}{3}$

7. $\frac{4}{5}$ ◯ $\frac{5}{10}$

8. $\frac{6}{10}$ ◯ $\frac{7}{8}$

9. **Number Sense** Kelvin says that $\frac{22}{30}$ is greater than $\frac{22}{32}$. Do you agree? Explain.

_____

_____

_____

_____

10. Jane bought $\frac{3}{5}$ lb of apples. Jack bought $\frac{2}{7}$ lb of apples. Who bought more pounds of apples? _____

11. Lyman and Amalia each painted part of the garage and their dad painted the rest. Lyman painted $\frac{2}{6}$ of the garage. Amalia painted $\frac{2}{8}$ of the garage. Who painted more? _____

Test Prep

12. Which of the fractions is less than $\frac{1}{3}$?

   A. $\frac{2}{7}$ B. $\frac{2}{6}$ C. $\frac{2}{3}$ D. $\frac{3}{4}$

13. **Writing in Math** How do you know $\frac{72}{80}$ is greater than $\frac{7}{8}$? Explain.

_____

_____

Name_____

Comparing and Ordering Fractions and Mixed Numbers

Compare. Write >, <, or = for each $\bigcirc$.

1. $\frac{6}{7}$ $\bigcirc$ $\frac{6}{8}$

2. $\frac{4}{9}$ $\bigcirc$ $\frac{2}{3}$

3. $1\frac{1}{10}$ $\bigcirc$ $1\frac{1}{12}$

4. $2\frac{4}{5}$ $\bigcirc$ $2\frac{5}{6}$

5. $3\frac{6}{9}$ $\bigcirc$ $3\frac{2}{3}$

6. $\frac{2}{5}$ $\bigcirc$ $\frac{2}{8}$

Order the numbers from least to greatest.

7. $\frac{4}{5}, \frac{4}{8}, \frac{3}{4}, \frac{5}{8}$ _____

8. $4\frac{1}{4}, 4\frac{1}{8}, 4\frac{10}{11}, 4\frac{2}{15}$ _____

9. $1\frac{3}{7}, 1\frac{3}{4}, 1\frac{2}{4}, 1\frac{8}{13}$ _____

10. Number Sense How do you know that $5\frac{1}{4}$ is less than $5\frac{4}{10}$?

_____

_____

11. A mechanic uses four wrenches to fix Mrs. Aaron's car. The wrenches are different sizes: $\frac{5}{16}$ in., $\frac{1}{2}$ in., $\frac{1}{4}$ in., and $\frac{7}{16}$ in. Order the sizes of the wrenches from greatest to least.

_____

Test Prep

12. Which is greater than $6\frac{1}{3}$?

A. $6\frac{1}{6}$ **B.** $6\frac{1}{5}$ **C.** $6\frac{1}{4}$ **D.** $6\frac{1}{2}$

13. Writing in Math Compare $3\frac{3}{22}$ and $3\frac{2}{33}$. Which is greater? How do you know?

_____

_____

_____

Name_____

Fractions and Decimals

Write a decimal and a fraction in simplest form for the
shaded portion of each model.

1.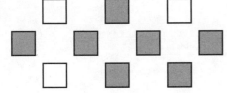

2.

_____   _____

Write each decimal as a fraction or mixed number in simplest form.

3. 2.25 _____   **4.** 3.74 _____

5. 0.08 _____   **6.** 0.375 _____

Write each fraction or mixed number as a decimal.

7. $\frac{2}{16}$ _____   **8.** $10\frac{3}{4}$ _____

9. $7\frac{2}{5}$ _____   **10.** $\frac{8}{40}$ _____

11. In Ron's school, 12 out of 30 students wear brown
shoes. Write the decimal that shows the portion
of students who wear brown shoes.   _____

Test Prep

12. Which is the decimal equivalent of the mixed number $3\frac{3}{6}$?

A. 3.36   **B.** 3.5   **C.** 3.56   **D.** 3.63

13. Writing in Math Explain how knowing that $5 \div 8 = 0.625$ helps
you find the decimal for $4\frac{5}{8}$.

_____

_____

_____

Fractions and Decimals on the Number Line

Show the set of numbers on the same number line. Then order the numbers from least to greatest.

1. 0.75, $\frac{8}{10}$, 0.2, $\frac{2}{5}$ _____

Write a fraction or mixed number in simplest form and a decimal that name each point.

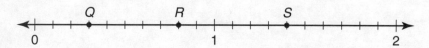

2. Point Q _____ **3.** Point R _____ **4.** Point S _____

5. Uma recorded the distances that volunteers walked in the charity event. Grace walked $1\frac{3}{5}$ mi, Wendell walked 1.3 mi, and Simon walked $1\frac{1}{10}$ mi. Show these amounts on a number line. Who walked the farthest?

_____

Test Prep

6. Which is a decimal that could go between the mixed numbers $4\frac{3}{5}$ and $4\frac{9}{10}$ on a number line?

  A. 4.45 **B.** 4.5 **C.** 4.75 **D.** 4.92

7. Writing in Math Explain how you know that 5.5 is to the right of $5\frac{1}{4}$ on the number line.

_____

Name_____

Use Logical Reasoning

Use the chart and logical reasoning to finish solving each problem.

1. Jenna, Mason, and Sean split the household tasks they
   had to do on Saturday. Their parents gave them a list of
   jobs: mow the lawn, wash the car, and do the laundry.
   Sean and Jenna do not want to mow the lawn. Mason
   helped Jenna fold the laundry when he was done with his
   job. Who did which task?

	Mow Lawn	Wash Car	Laundry
Jenna			
Mason			
Sean			

_____

_____

_____

2. Parker, Jaime, and Quincy need to choose a book to read for
   a school project. There are 3 kinds of books left and each
   student must choose a different kind of book. Jaime does
   not like science fiction. There are 4 consonants in the name
   of the student who chose mystery. Who chose which book?

	Mystery	Western	Science Fiction
Parker			
Jaime			
Quincy			

_____

_____

_____

Name_____

Helping the Birds

Simone's parents are bird-lovers. There is a birdhouse, some bird feeders, and a birdbath in their backyard. The family likes to watch the birds who come to enjoy the shelter, food, and water.

1. Simone's brother, Randy, says that he saw 12 birds today, and 6 of the birds were blue jays. Write the portion of the birds that were blue jays as a fraction and a decimal.

    _____

2. Simone and her mother went to the store to buy food for the bird feeders. They bought three different kinds of food. They bought $9\frac{3}{4}$ lb of one kind of food, 9.52 lb of another kind of food, and $9\frac{5}{12}$ lb of a third kind of food. Order the weights of the food from least to greatest.

    _____

3. Simone, Randy, and Kylie needed to clean and prepare the birdhouse, birdbath, and bird feeders for the winter. Randy does not like to clean the birdbath. Simone does the same job every year. Kylie cleaned the birdhouse. Who cleaned what?

	Birdhouse	Birdbath	Bird Feeders
Simone			
Randy			
Kylie			

    _____

    _____

    _____

    _____

Name_____

Adding and Subtracting Fractions with Like Denominators

Add or subtract. Simplify if possible.

1. $\frac{10}{12}$
    $+ \frac{8}{12}$
    _____

2. $\frac{8}{9}$
    $- \frac{5}{9}$
    _____

3. $\frac{7}{10}$
    $+ \frac{2}{10}$
    _____

4. $\frac{2}{3}$
    $- \frac{1}{3}$
    _____

5. $\frac{6}{8} + \frac{5}{8} + \frac{3}{8} = $ _____

6. $\frac{8}{10} - \frac{3}{10} = $ _____

7. $\frac{1}{4} + \frac{2}{4} + \frac{3}{4} = $ _____

8. $\frac{9}{11} - \frac{1}{11} = $ _____

9. $\frac{2}{5} + \frac{2}{5} + \frac{3}{5} = $ _____

10. $\frac{7}{8} - \frac{3}{8} = $ _____

11. **Number Sense** What fraction could you add to $\frac{4}{7}$ to get a sum greater than 1?

_____

12. **Reasoning** Write three fractions, using 10 as the denominator, whose sum is 1.

_____

Test Prep

13. Which of the following represents the difference between two equal fractions?

    A. 1   **B.** $\frac{1}{2}$ **C.** $\frac{1}{4}$ **D.** 0

14. **Writing in Math** In one night, George reads 3 chapters of a book with 27 chapters. After the second night, he has read a total of $\frac{8}{27}$ of the book. Explain how you would determine the number of chapters George read the second night. Solve the problem.

_____

_____

Understanding Adding and Subtracting with Unlike Denominators

Find each sum or difference. Simplify the answer, if possible.
You may use fraction strips or draw pictures to help.

1. $\frac{10}{12} - \frac{1}{4} =$ _____

2. $\frac{9}{10} - \frac{3}{5} =$ _____

3. $\frac{2}{9} + \frac{1}{3} =$ _____

4. $\frac{3}{4} + \frac{4}{5} =$ _____

5. $\frac{5}{6} + \frac{4}{9} =$ _____

6. $\frac{7}{8} - \frac{2}{6} =$ _____

7. $\frac{1}{6} + \frac{5}{12} =$ _____

8. $\frac{7}{12} - \frac{1}{4} =$ _____

9. **Number Sense** Which equivalent fraction would you
have to use in order to add $\frac{3}{5}$ to $\frac{21}{25}$? _____

Jeremy collected nickels for one week. He is making stacks of
his nickels to determine how many he has. The thickness of one
nickel is $\frac{1}{4}$ in.

10. How tall is a stack of 4 nickels? _____

11. What is the combined height of 3 nickels,
2 nickels, and 1 nickel? _____

12. How much taller is a stack of 3 nickels
than 1 nickel? _____

Test Prep

13. Which fraction is greatest?

    A. $\frac{5}{6}$ **B.** $\frac{7}{9}$ **C.** $\frac{2}{3}$ **D.** $\frac{9}{12}$

14. **Writing in Math** Explain why you cannot add fractions
with unlike denominators.

_____

_____

_____

Name_____

Adding Mixed Numbers

Estimate the sum first. Then add. Simplify, if necessary.

1. $7\frac{2}{3} + 8\frac{5}{6}$ _____

2. $4\frac{3}{4} + 2\frac{2}{5}$ _____

3. $11\frac{9}{10} + 3\frac{1}{20}$ _____

4. $7\frac{6}{7} + 5\frac{2}{7}$ _____

5. $5\frac{8}{9} + 3\frac{1}{2}$ _____

6. $21\frac{11}{12} + 17\frac{2}{3}$ _____

7. Number Sense Write two mixed numbers with a sum of 3.

_____

8. What is the total measure of an average man's brain and heart in kilograms?

Vital Organ Measures

Average woman's brain	$1\frac{3}{10}$ kg	$2\frac{4}{5}$ lb
Average man's brain	$1\frac{2}{5}$ kg	3 lb
Average human heart	$\frac{3}{10}$ kg	$\frac{7}{10}$ lb

_____

9. What is the total weight of an average woman's brain and heart in pounds? _____

10. What is the sum of the measures of an average man's brain and an average woman's brain in kilograms? _____

Test Prep

11. Which is a good comparison of the estimated sum and the actual sum of $7\frac{7}{8} + 2\frac{11}{12}$?

A. Estimated < actual

B. Actual > estimated

C. Actual = estimated

D. Estimated > actual

12. Writing in Math Can the sum of two mixed numbers be equal to 2? Explain why or why not.

_____

_____

_____

Subtracting Mixed Numbers

Estimate the difference first. Then subtract.
Simplify, if necessary.

1. $10\frac{3}{4}$
   $-\ 7\frac{1}{4}$

2. $7\frac{3}{7}$
   $-\ 2\frac{8}{21}$

3. 3
   $-\ 2\frac{2}{3}$

4. $17\frac{7}{8}$
   $-\ 12\frac{3}{12}$

5. $9\frac{5}{9} - 6\frac{5}{6}$ _____

6. $4\frac{3}{4} - 2\frac{2}{3}$ _____

7. $6\frac{1}{4} - 3\frac{1}{3}$ _____

8. $5\frac{1}{5} - 3\frac{7}{8}$ _____

9. $8\frac{2}{7} - 7\frac{1}{3}$ _____

10. $2\frac{9}{10} - 2\frac{1}{3}$ _____

The table shows the length
and width of several kinds of
bird eggs.

11. How much longer is the
    Canada goose egg than the
    raven egg?

    _____

Egg Sizes

Bird	Length	Width
Canada goose	$3\frac{2}{5}$ in.	$2\frac{3}{10}$ in.
Robin	$\frac{3}{4}$ in.	$\frac{3}{5}$ in.
Turtledove	$1\frac{1}{5}$ in.	$\frac{9}{10}$ in.
Raven	$1\frac{9}{10}$ in.	$1\frac{3}{10}$ in.

12. How much wider is the turtledove egg than
    the robin egg?   _____

Test Prep

13. Which is the difference of $21\frac{5}{16} - 18\frac{3}{4}$?

    A. $2\frac{7}{16}$ B. $2\frac{9}{16}$ C. $3\frac{7}{16}$ D. $3\frac{9}{16}$

14. **Writing in Math** Explain why it is necessary to rename $4\frac{1}{4}$ if
    you subtract $\frac{3}{4}$ from it.

    _____

    _____

    _____

Name_____

Work Backward

Solve each problem by working backward. Write the answers in complete sentences.

Barbara is refilling her bird feeders and squirrel feeders in her yard.

1. After filling her bird feeders, Barbara has $3\frac{1}{2}$ c of mixed birdseed left. The two feeders in the front yard took $4\frac{1}{2}$ c each. The two feeders in the backyard each took $2\frac{3}{4}$ c. The two feeders next to the living room window each took $3\frac{1}{4}$ c. How much mixed birdseed did Barbara have before filling the feeders?

   _____

2. After Barbara fills each of her 4 squirrel feeders with $2\frac{2}{3}$ c of peanuts, she has $1\frac{3}{4}$ c of peanuts left. How many cups of peanuts did Barbara start with?

   _____

Angela is knitting a scarf for her grandmother. Every day she knits a little bit more. The finished scarf will be 36 in. long.

3. Angela's mother starts knitting the scarf to help get her started. Angela knits a $6\frac{1}{2}$ in. section each day. After 5 days, the scarf is done. How many inches did Angela's mother knit?

   _____

4. How many more days would Angela have to knit to make the scarf 48 in. long?

   _____

Clint spends $\frac{1}{2}$ hr practicing trumpet, $\frac{3}{4}$ hr doing tasks around the house, $1\frac{1}{2}$ hr doing homework, and $\frac{1}{4}$ hr cleaning his room. He is finished at 7:30 P.M.

5. When did Clint start?

   _____

Name_____

Multiplying Fractions by Whole Numbers

P 8-10

Find each product.

1. $\frac{1}{4}$ of 96 = _____ 2. $\frac{4}{7}$ of 28 = _____ 3. $\frac{3}{4} \times 72$ = _____

4. $45 \times \frac{3}{9}$ = _____ 5. $56 \times \frac{7}{8}$ = _____ 6. $42 \times \frac{3}{7}$ = _____

7. $\frac{1}{2}$ of 118 = _____ 8. $\frac{3}{8}$ of 56 = _____ 9. $\frac{1}{10} \times 400$ = _____

10. $84 \times \frac{1}{6}$ = _____ 11. $64 \times \frac{5}{16}$ = _____ 12. $40 \times \frac{11}{20}$ = _____

13. $\frac{5}{8}$ of 48 = _____ 14. $\frac{1}{7}$ of 77 = _____ 15. $\frac{4}{5} \times 90$ = _____

16. $42 \times \frac{3}{14}$ = _____ 17. $72 \times \frac{5}{8}$ = _____ 18. $18 \times \frac{2}{3}$ = _____

19. $\frac{5}{6} \times 84$ = _____ 20. $\frac{11}{12} \times 144$ = _____ 21. $\frac{6}{7} \times 42$ = _____

22. **Patterns** Complete the table by writing the product of each expression in the box below it. Use a pattern to find each product. Explain the pattern.

$\frac{1}{2} \times 32$	$\frac{1}{4} \times 32$	$\frac{1}{8} \times 32$	$\frac{1}{16} \times 32$

_____

23. **Reasoning** If $\frac{1}{2}$ of 1 is $\frac{1}{2}$, what is $\frac{1}{2}$ of 2, 3, and 4? _____

Test Prep

24. Which is $\frac{2}{3}$ of 225?

   A. 75   **B.** 113   **C.** 150   **D.** 450

25. **Writing in Math** Explain why $\frac{1}{2}$ of 2 equals one whole.

_____

_____

Estimating Products of Fractions

Estimate each product.

1. $\frac{7}{8} \times 57$ _____

2. $\frac{3}{8} \times 28$ _____

3. $\frac{8}{9} \times 27$ _____

4. $24 \times \frac{2}{7}$ _____

5. $80 \times \frac{4}{7}$ _____

6. $\frac{5}{7} \times 50$ _____

7. $\frac{1}{8} \times 46$ _____

8. $\frac{2}{7} \times 58$ _____

9. $\frac{4}{9} \times 70$ _____

10. $18 \times \frac{3}{5}$ _____

11. $91 \times \frac{1}{10}$ _____

12. $\frac{3}{4} \times 39$ _____

13. About how many furlongs is $\frac{2}{3}$ of 1 mi?

_____

14. About how many rods is $\frac{4}{7}$ of 1 furlong?

_____

Distance Measurements

40 rods	=	1 furlong
8 furlongs	=	1 mi
3 mi	=	1 league
5,280 ft	=	1 mi

15. About how many miles is $\frac{7}{9}$ of 1 league?

_____

16. About how many feet is $\frac{23}{48}$ of 1 mi?

_____

17. **Number Sense** Is the product of $\frac{3}{9} \times 100$ greater than or less than 30? Explain.

_____

_____

Test Prep

18. Which is the most reasonable estimate for $55 \times \frac{5}{7}$?

   A. 30   **B.** 35   **C.** 55   **D.** 60

19. **Writing in Math** Which is easier, finding $\frac{2}{7}$ of 65 or $\frac{2}{7}$ of 63? Explain your answer.

_____

_____

Name_____

Multiplying Fractions

Write the multiplication problem that each model represents.

1.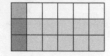

2.

_____   _____

Find each product. Simplify, if necessary.

3. $\frac{7}{8} \times \frac{4}{5} =$ _____

4. $\frac{3}{7} \times \frac{2}{3} =$ _____

5. $\frac{1}{6} \times \frac{2}{5} =$ _____

6. $\frac{2}{7} \times \frac{1}{4} =$ _____

7. $\frac{2}{9} \times \frac{1}{2} =$ _____

8. $\frac{3}{4} \times \frac{1}{3} =$ _____

9. $\frac{3}{8} \times \frac{4}{9} =$ _____

10. $\frac{1}{5} \times \frac{5}{6} =$ _____

11. $\frac{2}{3} \times \frac{5}{6} \times \frac{1}{4} =$ _____

12. $\frac{1}{2} \times \frac{1}{3} \times \frac{1}{4} =$ _____

13. **Algebra** If $\frac{4}{5} \times$ ■ $= \frac{2}{5}$, what is ■? _____

14. Ms. Shoemaker's classroom has 35 desks arranged in 5 by 7 rows. How many students does Ms. Shoemaker have in her class if there are $\frac{6}{7} \times \frac{4}{5}$ desks occupied?

_____

Test Prep

15. Which does the model represent?

A. $\frac{3}{8} \times \frac{3}{5}$ B. $\frac{3}{5} \times \frac{5}{8}$

C. $\frac{7}{8} \times \frac{2}{5}$ D. $\frac{4}{8} \times \frac{3}{5}$

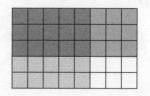

16. **Writing in Math** Describe a model that represents $\frac{3}{3} \times \frac{4}{4}$.

_____

_____

Name_____

Choose an Operation

Draw a picture to show the main idea.
Then choose an operation to solve the problem.

About one-third of all solid waste in the United
States comes from packaging materials.

Material Components of Packaging Waste

Material	Percentage
Paper	$47\frac{7}{10}$%
Glass	$24\frac{1}{2}$%
Plastic	■%
Steel	$6\frac{1}{2}$%
Wood	■%
Aluminum	$2\frac{1}{3}$%

1. The total percentage of packaging waste
   from plastic and paper is $62\frac{1}{5}$%. What is the
   percentage of plastic?

   _____

2. What is the combined total percentage
   of paper and glass in packaging waste?

   _____

3. The sum of the percentage from steel,
   aluminum, and wood is $13\frac{1}{3}$%.
   What is the percentage from wood?

   _____

4. If $27\frac{5}{6}$ tons of paper waste were
   produced in 1 year, how many tons
   of paper waste would be produced
   in 5 years?

   _____

Name_____

Natural Facts

Solve. Write your answers in complete sentences.

The skin is considered the heaviest
and largest organ of the human body.
The table lists some interesting facts about
the thickness of the skin.

Skin Facts	
Average thickness	$\frac{2}{25}$ in.
Thickest (upper back)	$\frac{1}{5}$ in.
Thinnest (eyelids)	$\frac{1}{50}$ in.

1. How many eyelids have an equal
   thickness to the skin on the upper back?

_____

2. What is the difference in thickness between the average
   thickness of the skin and the thickness of the skin on the eyelid?

_____

3. How much thicker is the skin on the upper back than the
   skin of the eyelid?

_____

The table at the right shows the percentage
of some elements in the human body.

The Human Body	
Element	**Percentage**
Carbon	$18\frac{1}{2}\%$
Hydrogen	$9\frac{1}{2}\%$
Nitrogen	$3\frac{1}{3}\%$
Calcium	$1\frac{1}{2}\%$
Phosphorous	1%

4. What percentage of the human body do
   carbon and hydrogen make up?

_____

_____

5. How much greater is the percentage of calcium and
   nitrogen combined than the percentage of phosphorus?

_____

_____

Name_____

Customary Units of Length

Complete.

1. 12 yd = _____ in.

2. 30 ft = _____ yd

3. 75 ft = _____ in.

4. 10 ft 7 in = _____ in.

5. 6 mi = _____ ft

6. 2 mi = _____ yd

7.   32 yd 2 ft
   +   4 yd 3 ft

8.   6 mi 10 yd
   −   4 mi 9 yd

9.   18 ft 4 in.
   + 22 ft 9 in.

The Statue of Liberty was a gift to the United States from the people of France. Some of the dimensions of the statue are shown here.

Measurements of the Statue of Liberty

Height from base of statue to the torch	151 ft 1 in.
Length of hand	16 ft 5 in.
Length of index finger	8 ft
Length of nose	4 ft 6 in.
Thickness of right arm	12 ft

10. What is the height, from the base of the statue to the torch, in inches? _____

11. What is the thickness of the statue's right arm in yards? _____

Test Prep

12. Which is equal to 435 in.?

    A. 37 ft   **B.** 36 ft   **C.** 12 yd 3 in.   **D.** 12 ft 3 in.

13. **Writing in Math** Explain how you can find the number of feet in 40 yd.

_____

_____

Measuring with Fractions of an Inch

Measure each segment to the nearest inch, $\frac{1}{2}$ inch, $\frac{1}{4}$ inch, and $\frac{1}{8}$ inch.

1. ⊢————————————⊣

_____

2. ⊢——————————⊣

_____

Use your ruler to draw a line segment of each length.

3. $\frac{3}{4}$ in.

4. $2\frac{1}{8}$ in.

5. **Reasoning** Sarah gave the same answer when asked to round $4\frac{7}{8}$ in. to the nearest $\frac{1}{2}$ inch and the nearest inch. Explain why Sarah is correct.

_____

_____

6. A real car is 18 times larger than a model car. If the model car is $5\frac{1}{4}$ in. long, how long is the real car? _____

Test Prep

7. What is the length of the segment?   ⊢—————————⊣

   A. $1\frac{7}{8}$ in.   **B.** $1\frac{3}{4}$ in.   **C.** $1\frac{1}{2}$ in.   **D.** 1 in.

8. **Writing in Math** If a line is measured as $1\frac{4}{8}$ in. long, explain how you could simplify the measurement.

_____

_____

Metric Units of Length

Which unit would be most appropriate for each measurement?
Write mm, cm, m, or km.

1. height of a basketball hoop   _____

2. distance from Chicago to Miami   _____

Measure each segment to the nearest centimeter and to the nearest millimeter.

3. ├───────────────────┤

_____

4. ├──────────┤

_____

Complete each sentence with mm, cm, m, or km.

5. A classroom is about 11 _____ wide.

6. A pencil is about 18 _____ long.

Some of the events at an upcoming track and field
meet are shown at the right.

7. In which event or events do athletes travel
more than a kilometer?

_____

Track and Field Events
50 m dash
1,500 m dash
400 m dash
100 m dash

8. In which event or events do athletes travel less than a kilometer?

_____

Test Prep

9. Which is the correct measurement of the line segment? ├──────────┤

A. 410 mm   **B.** 4.1 cm   **C.** 44 mm   **D.** 4 km

10. **Writing in Math** List one item in your classroom you would
measure using centimeters and one item in the classroom
you would measure using meters.

Converting Metric Units
Using Decimals

Find each equal measure.

1. 25 m = _____ dam

2. 4.5 m = _____ cm

3. 200 hm = _____ m

4. 987 mm = _____ cm

5. 4.2 km = _____ m

6. 0.35 dm = _____ mm

7. 345 cm = _____ m

8. 10 m = _____ mm

9. Number Sense List three measurements with different
units equal to 5 m.

_____

Mount St. Helens, a volcano in the state of Washington, erupted
on May 18, 1980. Before the eruption, Mount St. Helens was
2,950 m high. After the eruption, it was 2,550 m high.

10. What is the difference in height of Mount St. Helens
before and after the eruption expressed in meters?   _____

11. Before the eruption, how many kilometers high was
Mount St. Helens?   _____

12. After the eruption, how many hectometers high was
Mount St. Helens?   _____

Test Prep

13. Which measurement is equal to 10 dam?

    A. 100 hm   **B.** 1 m   **C.** 0.1 hm   **D.** 100 m

14. Writing in Math Explain how you would convert 4 m to millimeters.

_____

_____

Name_____

Finding Perimeter

Find the perimeter of each figure.

1. 3 cm ◁ 3 cm
5 cm

2. 7 km
7 km ⬜ 7 km
7 km

3. 1 m
2 m ⬡ 3 m
2 m 2 m
1 m

4. 7.5 hm
5 hm ▱ 5 hm
7.5 hm

_____ _____ _____ _____

5. Number Sense What is the perimeter of a square if
one of the sides is 3 mi?

_____

The dimensions of a football field
are shown at the right.

6. What is the perimeter of the entire
football field including the
end zones?

_____

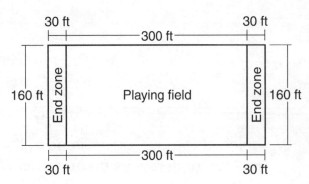

7. What is the perimeter of each end zone?

_____

Test Prep

8. What is the perimeter of this figure?

A. 18 m   **B.** 15 m

C. 12 ft   **D.** 10 ft

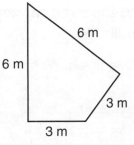

9. Writing in Math A square has a perimeter of 12 m. How
many possible lengths are there for each side? List them
and explain your answer.

_____

_____

_____

Name_____

Finding Circumference

Find each circumference. Use 3.14 for π.

1.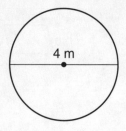
4 m

2.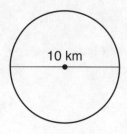
10 km

3.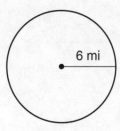
6 mi

_____   _____   _____

4. $d = 7$ hm   **5.** $r = 7$ in.   **6.** $r = 9$ km

_____   _____   _____

7. $d = 2$ in.   **8.** $d = 8$ cm   **9.** $d = 6$ yd

_____   _____   _____

10. Which of the U.S. coins listed in the table have circumferences greater than 68 mm?

Coin	Diameter
Penny	19.05 mm
Nickel	21.21 mm
Dime	17.91 mm
Quarter	24.26 mm
Half-dollar	30.61 mm
Dollar	26.5 mm

_____

For 11 and 12, round the circumference to the nearest hundredth millimeter.

What is the circumference of a

11. penny? _____   **12.** dime? _____

Test Prep

13. Which pair correctly shows the diameter and circumference of a circle?

    A. $d = 10$ m, $C = 15.7$ m   **B.** $d = 10$ m, $C = 31.4$ m

    C. $d = 10$ m, $C = 50$ m   **D.** $d = 10$ m, $C = 7.85$ m

14. Writing in Math Could you find the circumference of a circle using the exact value for π? Why or why not?

_____

Name_____

Finding Area

Find the area of each figure.

1.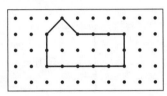

2.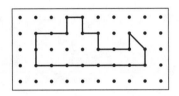

3.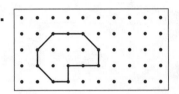

_____   _____   _____

On each dot paper, draw a shape with each given area.

4. 7 square units

5. $5\frac{1}{2}$ square units

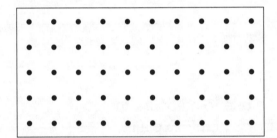

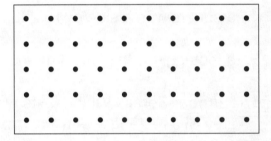

6. Tara was asked to draw a figure with an area of 11 square units. Is her drawing correct? If not, what is the area of the figure she drew?

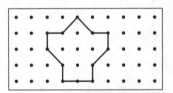

_____

Test Prep

7. Which is the area of this figure?

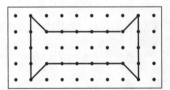

    A. 17 square units   **B.** 16 square units

    C. 15 square units   **D.** 14 square units

8. **Writing in Math** Can shapes with the same area have different perimeters? Explain.

_____

_____

_____

Name _____

Areas of Squares and Rectangles

Find the area of each figure.

1.

$l = 4$ cm

$w = 3$ cm

_____

2.

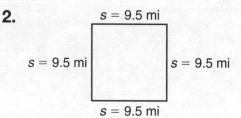

$s = 9.5$ mi

$s = 9.5$ mi $s = 9.5$ mi

$s = 9.5$ mi

_____

3. a rectangle with sides 6.5 km and 3.4 km   _____

4. a square with a side of 10.2 ft   _____

5. a rectangle with sides 9 m and 9.2 m   _____

6. Number Sense Which units would you use to measure the
area of a rectangle with $l = 1$ m and $w = 34$ cm? Explain.

_____

_____

Test Prep

7. Which of the following shapes has an area of 34 ft^2?

A. A square with $s = 8.5$ m

B. A rectangle with $l = 15$ ft, $w = 2$ ft

C. A square with $s = 16$ ft

D. A rectangle with $l = 17$ ft, $w = 2$ ft

8. Writing in Math The area of a square is 49 m^2. What is the
length of one of its sides? Explain how you solved this problem.

_____

_____

_____

Name_____

Areas of Parallelograms

Find the area of each parallelogram.

1.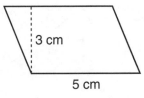

3 cm

5 cm

_____

2.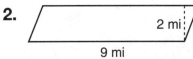

2 mi

9 mi

_____

3.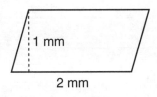

1 mm

2 mm

_____

4.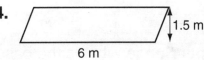

1.5 m

6 m

_____

Algebra Find the missing measurement for the parallelogram.

5. $A = 34\ \text{in}^2$, $b = 17$ in., $h =$ _____

6. List three sets of base and height measurements for parallelograms with areas of 40 square units.

_____

_____

Test Prep

7. Which is the height of the parallelogram?

A. 55 m   **B.** 55.5 m

C. 5 m   **D.** 5.5 m

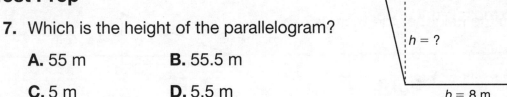

$A = 44\ \text{m}^2$

$h = ?$

$b = 8$ m

8. Writing in Math What are a possible base and height for a parallelogram with an area of 45 ft^2? Explain how you solved this problem.

_____

_____

Name_____

Areas of Triangles

Find the area of each triangle.

1.

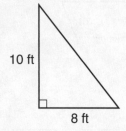

10 ft

8 ft

2.

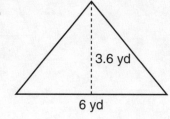

3.6 yd

6 yd

3.

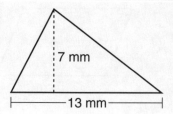

7 mm

13 mm

_____ _____ _____

4. **Number Sense** What is the base measurement of
   a triangle with an area of 30 m² and a height of 10 m? _____

Algebra Find the missing measurement for each triangle.

5. $A = 36\ mi^2$, $b =$ _____, $h = 12$ mi

6. $A =$ _____, $b = 12$ mm, $h = 7.5$ mm

7. List three sets of base and height measurements for
   triangles with areas of 30 square units.

_____

_____

Test Prep

8. Which is the height of the triangle?

   A. 4.5 ft   **B.** 6 ft

   C. 8 ft   **D.** 9 ft

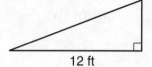

$A = 27\ ft^2$

12 ft

9. **Writing in Math** Can you find the base and height
   measurements for a triangle if you know that the area is
   22 square units? Explain why or why not.

_____

_____

PROBLEM-SOLVING STRATEGY
Draw a Picture

Solve. Write the answer in a complete sentence.

1. Erica painted a picture of her dog. The picture has an area
    of 3,600 cm^2 and is a square. She has placed the picture in
    a frame that is 5 cm wide. What is the perimeter of the
    picture frame?

    _____

    _____

2. The new playground at Middledale School will be enclosed
    by a fence. The playground will be a square and will have
    an area of 225 yd^2. The number of yards on each side will
    be a whole number. What is the least amount of fencing
    that could be required to enclose the playground?

    _____

    _____

3. The floor in the back of Karl's truck is 6 ft long and has an
    area of 24 ft^2. Karl wants to haul as many boxes on the
    floor as possible. He cannot stack the boxes or they will fall
    out as he drives. If each square box is 2 ft long, how many
    boxes can Karl fit in the back of his truck?

    _____

    _____

Time

Find each equal measure.

1. 96 hr = _____ d

2. 343 d = _____ wk

3. 6 yr 9 d = _____ d

4. 1,416 hr = _____ d

5. 12 h 9 min = _____ sec

6. 3 yr 5 d = _____ hr

7. **Reasoning** Are there more days or weeks in a century? How do you know?

_____

_____

Information about the International Space Station is in the table.

Expedition Number	Time from Launching to Landing
Expedition One	138 d, 18 hr, 39 min
Expedition Two	167 d, 6 hr, 4 min

8. Express the length of Expedition One in hours and minutes.

_____

9. Express the length of Expedition Two in weeks, days, hours, and minutes.

_____

Test Prep

10. Which length of time is equivalent to 92 hr?

   A. 4 d   **B.** 331,200 min   **C.** 5,520 min   **D.** 3,200 sec

11. **Writing in Math** How many hours are in 43,200 sec? Explain how you solved this problem.

_____

_____

Name_____

Elapsed Time

Find each elapsed time.

1. 9:59 P.M. to 10:45 P.M. _____

2. 11:45 A.M. to 3:38 P.M. _____

3.

    A.M.   A.M.

_____

4.

         A.M.   P.M.

_____

Find the start time using the given elapsed time.

5. Start: 3:46 P.M   Elapsed: 2 hr 20 min   _____

6. Add.   2 hr 45 min
       + 3 hr 58 min

7. Add.   6 hr 47 min
       + 5 hr 28 min

The White House Visitor Center is open from 7:30 A.M. until 4:00 P.M.

8. Tara and Miguel got to the Visitor Center when it opened, and spent 1 hr 20 min there. At what time did they leave?

9. Jennifer left the Visitor Center at 3:30 P.M. after spending 40 min there. At what time did she arrive?

Test Prep

10. A football game lasted 2 hr 37 min. It finished at 4:22 P.M. When did it start?

    A. 1:45 P.M.   **B.** 1:55 P.M.   **C.** 2:45 P.M.   **D.** 2:50 P.M.

11. **Writing in Math** What is 1 hour and 35 minutes before 4:05 P.M.? Explain how you solved this problem.

_____

Name_____

Temperature

Write each temperature in Celsius and Fahrenheit.

1.

2.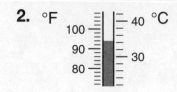

3.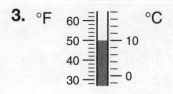

_____ , _____   _____ , _____   _____ , _____

Find each change in temperature.

4. 34°F to 67°F _____   **5.** 12°C to 7°C _____

6. Number Sense Which is a smaller increase in temperature: a 5°F increase or a 5°C increase?

_____

Information about the record highest temperatures in four states is shown.

7. What is the difference between the record high temperature in Florida and the record high temperature in Alaska in °C?

_____

Record High Temperature

State	°F	°C
Alaska	100	38
Florida	109	43
Michigan	112	44
Hawaii	100	38

8. What is the difference between the record high temperature in Michigan and the record high temperature in Florida in °F?   _____

Test Prep

9. What is the difference between −6°C and 12°C?

A. 6°C   **B.** 12°C   **C.** 18°C   **D.** 19°C

10. Writing in Math Which is warmer, 1°F or 1°C? Explain how you found this answer.

_____

_____

Name_____

Writing to Explain

Write to explain.

1. How could you convert a measurement given in millimeters to kilometers?

_____

_____

_____

_____

2. How could you find the perimeter of a brick in this wall?

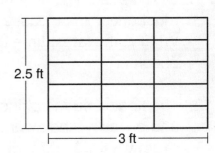

_____

_____

_____

_____

_____

_____

3. How could you find the height of this triangle?

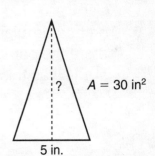

_____

_____

PROBLEM-SOLVING APPLICATIONS
Summer Parade

The parade-planning committee met to organize the summer parade. Here are some notes from the meeting.

Springdale Summer Parade

Planning Information:

Date of parade—June 5

Parade start time—1:30 P.M.

Maximum size of floats—12 ft x 20 ft

Parade may be canceled due to rain or temp less than 50°F

Parade route—5.2 km long

1. On parade day, the conductor of each marching band must check in at least 2 hr before the parade starts. What is the latest time the band conductors can check in?

   _____

2. The floats and marching groups will be judged, and prizes will be awarded. The judge's stand is exactly halfway through the parade route. How many meters from the beginning of the parade is the judge's stand?

   _____

3. If a rectangular parade float is the maximum allowed size, what is the area of the parade float?

   _____

4. The temperature on June 5 is 85°F. How many degrees greater than the minimum temperature for the parade is this?

   _____

5. The parade-planning committee met 6 weeks before the parade. How many days before the parade was this?

   _____

Solid Figures

What solid figure does each object resemble?

1.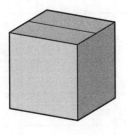

_____

2.

_____

3.

_____

4. Reasoning One of the faces of a polyhedron is a triangle.
What are two possible types of polyhedrons this might be?

_____

_____

Test Prep

5. Which term best describes the figure?

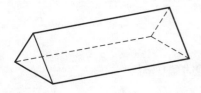

A. Cone

B. Triangular prism

C. Pyramid

D. Rectangular prism

6. Writing in Math How many vertices does a cone have? Explain.

_____

_____

_____

Name_____

Views of Solid Figures

1. What solid does the net represent?

_____

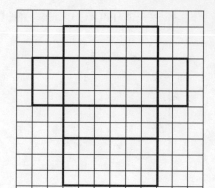

Draw the front, side, and
top views of the stack of
unit blocks.

2.

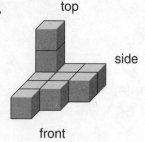

top

side

front

3. Reasoning How many blocks are not visible
in the figure at the right?

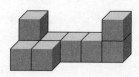

_____

Test Prep

4. If a net consists of 6 squares, what is a solid figure that
could be formed by it?

  A. Rectangular prism   **B.** Cone

  C. Pyramid   **D.** Cube

5. Writing in Math Draw a net for a triangular
pyramid. Explain how you know your diagram
is correct.

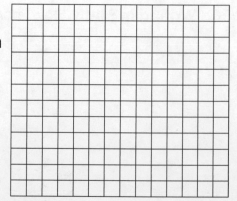

_____

_____

Name_____

Surface Area

Find the surface area of each rectangular prism.

1.
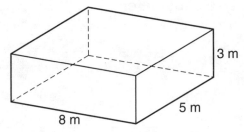
3 m
5 m
8 m

2.
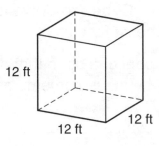
12 ft
12 ft
12 ft

_____   _____

Music and computer CDs are often stored in plastic cases
called jewel cases.

3. One size of jewel case is 140 mm × 120 mm × 4 mm.
What is the surface area of this jewel case?

_____

4. A jewel case that holds 2 CDs is 140 mm × 120 mm ×
9 mm. What is the surface area of this jewel case?

_____

Test Prep

5. What is the surface area of a rectangular prism with the
dimensions 3 in. by 4 in. by 8 in.?

A. 96 in²   **B.** 112 in²   **C.** 136 in²   **D.** 152 in²

6. Writing in Math Explain why the formula for finding the
surface area of a rectangular prism is helpful.

_____

_____

_____

_____

Name_____

Use Objects

Use Centimeter Cubes to Solve a Problem Use centimeter cubes to find the surface area.

1. Make a model of a cube that has a surface area of 54 cm². What are the measurements of the model?

   _____

2. Make a model of a rectangular prism that is not a cube and has a surface area of 62 cm². What are the measurements of this rectangular prism?

   _____

   _____

   _____

   _____

Use Cards to Solve a Problem Write the information on slips of paper to help solve the problem.

3. Yu-Li takes six classes each day. The classes are math, science, language arts, social studies, music, and physical education. Use the clues to figure out the order of the classes.
   - There is a class before and after social studies.
   - There is no class after music.
   - There is one class before math.
   - There are two classes between social studies and music.
   - Physical education is right after science.

   _____

   _____

   _____

Name_____

Volume

Find the volume of each rectangular prism.

1. base area 56 in^2, height 6 in. _____

2. base area 32 cm^2, height 12 cm _____

3. base area 42 m^2, height 8 m _____

4.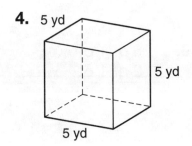
5 yd, 5 yd, 5 yd

_____

5.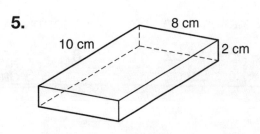
8 cm, 10 cm, 2 cm

_____

6. **Algebra** What is the height of a solid with a volume of 120 m^3 and base area of 30 m^2? _____

Michael bought some cereal at the grocery store.

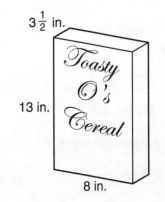
$3\frac{1}{2}$ in.
Toasty O's Cereal
13 in.
8 in.

7. What is the base area of the box?

_____

8. What is the volume of the box?

_____

Test Prep

9. What is the base area of this figure?

   A. 3.2 m^2 **B.** 32 m^2

   C. 320 m^2 **D.** 3,200 m^2

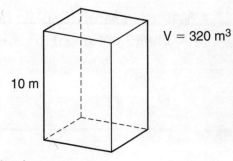
V = 320 m^3
10 m

10. **Writing in Math** Explain how you would find the base area of a rectangular prism if you know the volume and the height.

_____

Customary Units of Capacity

Complete.

1. 2 qt = _____ pt

2. 5 c = _____ pt _____ c

3. 3 gal = _____ pt

4. 2 fl oz = _____ tsp

5. 4 qt = _____ c

6. 9 pt = _____ c

Write each answer in simplest form.

7.   5 c 4 fl oz
  − 4 c 3 fl oz
  ‾‾‾‾‾‾‾‾‾‾‾

8.   7 gal 2 qt
  + 3 gal 1 qt
  ‾‾‾‾‾‾‾‾‾‾‾

9.   6 qt 1 pt
  + 2 qt 1 pt
  ‾‾‾‾‾‾‾‾‾‾

10. **Estimation** Estimate the number of tablespoons in 445 teaspoons.

_____

11. **Reasoning** If you needed only 1 c of milk, what is your best choice at the grocery store—a quart container, a pint container, or a $\frac{1}{2}$ gal container?

_____

Test Prep

12. Which of the following is equivalent to 1 c?

    A. 4 fl oz   **B.** 2 pt   **C.** 48 tsp   **D.** 32 tbsp

13. **Writing in Math** Explain how you would convert a measurement given in tablespoons into pints.

_____

_____

Metric Units of Capacity

Complete.

1. 5 L = _____ mL

2. 1,298 mL = _____ L

3. 3.4 L = _____ mL

4. 956 mL = _____ L

5. 82 mL = _____ L

6. 98 L = _____ mL

7. **Estimation** Which capacity is most reasonable for each object?

a. drinking glass
50 mL or 50 L

b. swimming pool
80,000 mL or 80,000 L

c. bottle cap
20 mL or 20 L

_____

_____

_____

8. Latoya's science fair experiment measured the rate at
which the temperature of water changed. She tested four
different-sized containers of water: 1 L, 2 L, 4 L, and 5 L.
Express these capacities in milliliters.

_____

Test Prep

9. Which of the following is equivalent to 2 mL?

A. 20 L   B. 0.2 L   C. 0.02 L   D. 0.002 L

10. **Writing in Math** Tell whether you would use multiplication
or division to convert milliliters to liters. Explain your
answer.

_____

_____

_____

_____

Name _____

Customary Units of Weight

Complete.

1. 200 lb = _____ T

2. 56 oz = _____ lb _____ oz

3. 2.5 lb = _____ oz

4. 4,000 lb = _____ T

5. 40 oz = _____ lb _____ oz

6. 90 lb = _____ oz

Write each answer in simplest form.

7.   5 lb 12 oz
     − 4 lb 13 oz

8.   7 T 200 lb
     +   1,900 lb

9.   29 lb 4 oz
     + 11 lb 13 oz

10. Estimation Estimate the number of ounces of potatoes in a 5 lb bag of potatoes. _____

11. Did you know that there is litter in outer space? Humans exploring space have left behind bags of trash, bolts, gloves, and pieces of satellites. There are currently about 4,000,000 lb of litter in orbit around Earth. About how many tons of space litter is this? _____

12. Karla bought 2 lb of red beads, $1\frac{3}{4}$ lb of green beads, and 10 oz of string at the craft store. How much did Karla's supplies weigh altogether? _____

Test Prep

13. Which of the following is equivalent to 92.5 lb?

    A. 1,472 oz   **B.** 1,480 oz   **C.** 1,479 oz   **D.** 1,488 oz

14. Writing in Math Explain the difference between 1 fl oz and 1 oz.

_____

_____

Name_____

Metric Units of Mass

Complete.

1. 20 kg = _____ g

2. 520 g = _____ kg

3. 0.189 kg = _____ g

4. 45 g = _____ mg

5. 1.45 kg = _____ g

6. 1,200 mg = _____ g

7. Number Sense Which has less mass, 800 g or 8 kg? _____

The list shows Jeffrey's grocery list.

1 box of pasta	454 g
1 can of soup	298 g
1 jar of peanut butter	1,130 g
1 box of cereal	432 g

8. Do any items on the list have a mass greater than 400,000 mg? If so, which ones?

_____

9. Do any items on the list have a mass less than 0.3 kg? If so, which ones?

_____

Test Prep

10. Which of the following is equivalent to 80 mg?

A. 8 g   **B.** 0.8 g   **C.** 0.08 g   **D.** 0.008 g

11. Writing in Math Which do you think is easier to convert, units of customary measurement or units of metric measurement? Explain your answer.

_____

Name_____

Exact Answer or Estimate

Tell whether an exact answer or an estimate is needed. Then solve each problem and check to see if your answer is reasonable.

1. Paper grocery bags hold between 9 and 10 kg of groceries. If Marie has placed items with a mass of 5.3 kg in a paper grocery bag, about how many more kilograms of groceries can she place in the bag?

   _____

2. The water cooler for the cross-country team holds 20 L of water. If each of the 25 runners has had 500 mL of water to drink from the cooler, exactly how much water is left in the cooler?

   _____

3. A recipe for lemonade calls for about 2 qt of ice water. How many pints of ice water are needed?

   _____

4.

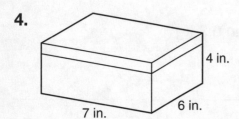

4 in.

6 in.

7 in.

   The third graders are painting shoe boxes in art class. If it takes Dominic 1 min to paint 4 in^2, how long will it take him to paint the outside of this box?

   _____

Name_____

Tropical Fish

Solve. Write your answer in a complete
sentence.

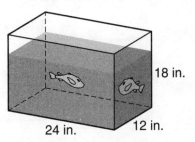

18 in.

24 in.   12 in.

1. Jerome works in a tropical fish store. Every
   day, he cleans the outside of the fish tanks
   with glass cleaner. The fish tanks do not
   have lids, and the bottoms of the fish tanks
   do not need to be cleaned. What is the total
   surface area Jerome must clean if there are
   50 fish tanks like the one shown here?

   _____

   _____

2. The fish tanks at the tropical fish store hold 20 gal of water
   each. How many quarts of water are in the 50 fish tanks at
   the store?

   _____

   _____

3. Jerome's job duties include feeding the fish. There are
   5 kinds of fish that he feeds: guppies, zebra danios, betas,
   platys, and neon tetras. Use the following clues to find the
   order in which Jerome feeds them.

   • Jerome feeds the guppies third.

   • Jerome does not feed the betas right before or right after
     the guppies.

   • Jerome feeds the zebra danios last.

   • Jerome feeds the platys after the betas.

   _____

   _____

   _____

Name_____

Understanding Ratios

Use the chart below in 1–5 to write each ratio three ways.

Mr. White's 3rd Grade Class (24 Students)

Gender:	Male	8	Female	16				
Eye Color:	Blue	6	Brown	4	Hazel	12	Green	2
Hair Color:	Blond	5	Red	1	Brown	15	Black	3

1. male students to female students _____

2. female students to male students _____

3. red-haired students to all students _____

4. all students to green-eyed students _____

5. Reasoning Is the ratio of male students to female students the same as the ratio of male students to all students? Explain.

_____

_____

Test Prep

6. George has 2 sons and 1 daughter. What is the ratio of daughters to sons?

A. 2 to 1   **B.** 1 to 2   **C.** 3:1   **D.** $\frac{2}{1}$

7. Writing in Math The ratio of blue beads to white beads in a necklace is 3:8. Nancy says that for every 11 beads, 3 are blue. Do you agree? Explain.

_____

_____

_____

Equal Ratios

Write each ratio in simplest form.

1. 9 to 3 _____

2. 2:12 _____

3. 20 to 45 _____

4. 16:80 _____

Give two other ratios that are equal to each.

5. 1 to 7 _____

6. $\frac{3}{9}$ _____

7. 4:3 _____

8. 9:24 _____

Are the ratios in each pair equal?

9. $\frac{1}{2}$ and $\frac{4}{8}$ _____

10. $\frac{16}{18}$ and $\frac{4}{6}$ _____

11. $\frac{1}{5}$ and $\frac{5}{30}$ _____

12. $\frac{10}{34}$ and $\frac{15}{51}$ _____

A cereal company has packaged a movie ticket in some of
its cereal boxes. In other boxes, there is either a plastic ring
or a puzzle. Out of 50 cereal boxes, there are 21 plastic rings,
28 puzzles, and 1 movie ticket.

13. If 200 boxes of cereal are produced, how
many have movie tickets in them? _____

14. What is the ratio of puzzles to total
boxes when there are 56 puzzles? _____

Test Prep

15. Which ratio is equal to 13:26?

A. 2:1   **B.** 1:3   **C.** 1:2   **D.** 1:7

16. **Writing in Math** Use the information from Exercises 13 and
14. Explain how you could find the total number of plastic
rings in cereal boxes if there are a total of 3 movie tickets.

_____

_____

Name_____

Graphs of Equal Ratios

1. A square has four angles. Complete this table of equal ratios.

Squares	1	2	3	4	5	6
Angles	4	8				

2. On the grid, graph the ordered pairs from the table. Connect them with a line.

3. If the line in Exercise 2 is extended, would it cross the point (10, 36)? Explain.

_____

_____

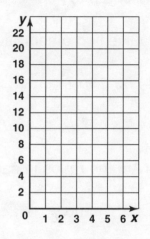

4. Give three equal ratios not shown that would be found on the line of the given graph.

_____

_____

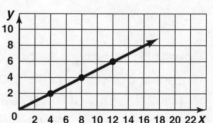

Test Prep

5. Which ordered pair will be found on the graph for the ratio 2:3?

   A. (3, 6)   **B.** (6, 4)   **C.** (4, 6)   **D.** (12, 16)

6. **Writing in Math** Does the given graph show a line that is more likely to be for ratios equal to 1:3 or 3:1? Explain.

   _____

   _____

   _____

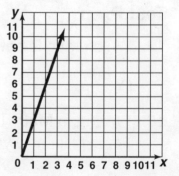

Name_____

Rates

Tell the two quantities being compared in each.

1. 32 mi per hour

_____

2. $16.00 each hour

_____

3. 32 cents per mile

_____

Write each rate as a unit rate.

4. 18 mi in 2 hr

_____

5. $60.00 for 5 blankets

_____

6. 300 beats in 2 min

_____

7. At a carnival for the school, you can purchase booth tickets
   in groups of 4 or 25. Four tickets cost $1, and 25 tickets
   cost $5. Which is a better buy? Use the unit rate to explain.

_____

_____

_____

Test Prep

8. Which rate is the best buy?

   A. $19 for 3 lb   **B.** $12 for 2 lb   **C.** $55 for 10 lb   **D.** $350 for 50 lb

9. **Writing in Math** Sharon says that she changed jobs
   because she gets paid a better rate now. Her old job paid
   her $8 per hour. Her new job pays her $300 per week.
   Sharon has worked 40 hr per week in each job. Does
   Sharon get paid a better rate for her new job? Explain.

_____

_____

Name_____

Make a Table

Solve. Write the answer in a complete sentence.

1. Brenda is making bracelets that each use three 6 in. strips of leather. She wants to make 6 bracelets. How many strips of leather does Brenda need?

   _____

   _____

2. Charles can type 72 words per minute. He needs to type a paper with 432 words. How many minutes will it take Charles to type the paper?

   _____

   _____

3. Samuel is building a brick wall. Each row has 15 bricks. Samuel has 75 bricks. How many rows of bricks can he build?

   _____

4. Maggie is taking her cats into the vet for their shots. The vet charges $18 for one shot and $16 for each shot after that. How much will it cost Maggie to get shots for all of her 6 cats?

   _____

   _____

5. A baseball team is ordering equipment for their practice sessions. For every 2 bats they order, they also order 9 balls. The coach decides to order 12 new baseball bats. How many balls did he order?

   _____

Scale Drawings

Refer to this scale drawing of a park.

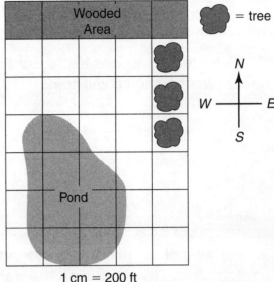

1 cm = 200 ft

1. What is the actual length of the pond from the north end to the south end?

_____

2. What is the actual width, from west to east, of the wooded area?

_____

3. A common highway map scale is 1 cm = 5 mi. If you were going to make a map that covered a distance of 900 mi wide, how wide would your map need to be?

_____

4. A garden plot is drawn to scale. The actual garden is 60 ft long and 20 ft wide. If you have a paper that is 1 ft long, what scale can you use to draw the plot as large as possible on the paper?

_____

Test Prep

5. In a scale drawing of a house that uses a scale of 5 mm = 3 ft, how tall will a house that is 27 ft tall appear on the drawing?

   A. 9 mm   **B.** 27 mm   **C.** 30 mm   **D.** 45 mm

6. **Writing in Math** David drew a scale drawing of an airplane. The actual airplane was 32 ft long and David's drawing was 8 in. long. Find the scale and explain.

_____

_____

_____

Name_____

Writing to Explain

Write to explain.

1. Use the juice prices to predict how much a 64 oz container of juice will cost.

   _____

   _____

   _____

$0.40 $1.60

2. Isabel took 20 min to run around the track 6 times. John took 3 min to run around the track once. Which student was running faster?

   _____

   _____

3. Nancy is saving $2 from her allowance every week. Marco is saving $1 the first week, $2 the second week, $3 the third week, and so on. At the end of 10 weeks, who will have saved more money? How much more?

   _____

   _____

4. **Reasonableness** For every 3 cans of vegetables purchased, you get 1 free can. Tessie went home with 32 cans of vegetables, but only had to pay for 16. Is this correct? Explain.

   _____

   _____

   _____

   _____

Understanding Percent

Write the fraction in lowest terms and the percent that
represents the shaded part of each figure.

1.
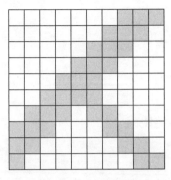

2.
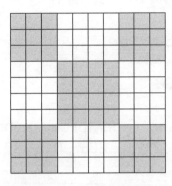

_____   _____

3. In the square, if part A is $\frac{1}{4}$ of the square
and part C is $\frac{1}{10}$ of the square, what percent
of the square is part B?

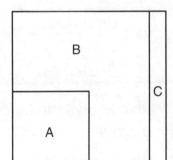

_____

4. In Russia, $\frac{1}{4}$ of the land is covered by forests.
What percent of Russia is covered by forest?
What percent of Russia is not covered by forest?

_____

5. In the United States, $\frac{3}{10}$ of the land is forests and
woodland. What percent of the United States
is forest and woodland?

_____

Test Prep

6. If $\frac{2}{5}$ of a figure is shaded, what percent is not shaded?

A. 20%   **B.** 30%   **C.** 50%   **D.** 60%

7. Writing in Math Explain how a decimal is related
to a percent.

_____

_____

Mental Math: Finding a Percent of a Number

Find each using mental math.

1. 20% of 60 _____

2. 30% of 500 _____

3. 25% of 88 _____

4. 70% of 30 _____

5. **Reasoning** Order these numbers from least to greatest.
   0.85, $\frac{1}{4}$, 72%, $\frac{5}{8}$, 20%, 0.3

_____

	Rural	Urban
Bermuda	0%	100%
Cuba	25%	75%
Guatemala	60%	40%

The table shows the percent of the population that live in rural and urban areas of each country.

6. Out of every 300 people in Cuba, how many
   of them live in a rural area?   _____

7. Out of every 1,000 people in Guatemala,
   how many live in urban areas?   _____

Test Prep

8. What is 40% of 240?

   A. 48   **B.** 96   **C.** 128   **D.** 960

9. **Writing in Math** If there are 1,241,356 people who live in
   Bermuda, how many residents of Bermuda live in urban
   areas? How many live in rural areas? Explain your answer.

_____

_____

_____

Name_____

Estimating Percents

Estimate.

1. 52% of 420 _____
2. 68% of 70 _____
3. 11% of 120 _____

4. 76% of 81 _____
5. 39% of 31 _____
6. 27% of 24 _____

7. 9% of 72 _____
8. 58% of 492 _____
9. 18% of 402 _____

10. **Algebra** Use estimation to find the value of x when 25% of x is about 30.

_____

A group of students were surveyed on what they like to do after school. There were 200 students surveyed, and the results were graphed.

11. Estimate the number of students who prefer to play a sport after school.

_____

12. Do more than or fewer than 40 students prefer to read after school?

_____

Test Prep

13. Which is the best estimation for 31% of 68?

   A. 20   **B.** 21   **C.** 25   **D.** 27

14. **Writing in Math** Linda says that 42 is a reasonable estimate for 34% of 119. Is she correct? Explain why or why not.

_____

_____

_____

Name_____

A Pack of Percents

Solve. Write your answer to each in a complete sentence.

1. A bookstore charges 12% of your purchase price to cover
   sales tax and shipping and handling. About how much will
   be added to your purchase price if your order totals $216?

   _____

2. In Derreck's class, 3 out of every 7 students are girls. If there are
   16 boys in Derreck's class, how many of the students are girls?

   _____

3. Complete the table to help you find how many blocks are
   needed if a tower is built of blocks where each row has one
   less block than the one below it. The tower is 8 rows high,
   and the bottom row has 20 blocks in it.

Rows	1	2	3	4	5	6	7	8
Blocks Needed								

   _____

   _____

4. Kinsey ran 3 laps around the track in 12 min yesterday.
   Today she ran 5 laps, and it took her 19 min 20 sec. Which
   day did Kinsey run faster?

   _____

5. It costs $0.89 for 1 L of spring water, and a 5 L jug of
   spring water costs $4.95. Which is the better buy?

   _____

   _____

Name_____

The Coordinate Plane

Write the ordered pair for each point.

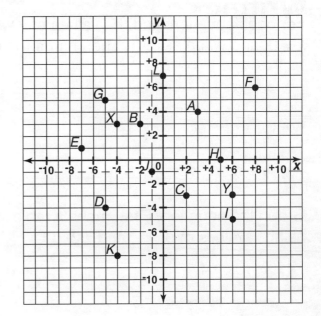

1. A _____

2. B _____

3. C _____

4. D _____

5. E _____

6. F _____

Name the point for each ordered pair.

7. (+5, 0) _____   **8.** (−1, −1) _____   **9.** (0, +7) _____

10. (+6, −5)_____   **11.** (−4, −8) _____   **12.** (−5, +5)_____

13. If a taxi cab were to start at the point (0, 0) and drive
6 units left, 3 units down, 1 unit right, and 9 units up,
what ordered pair would name the point the cab
would finish at?   _____

Test Prep

14. Use the coordinate graph above. Which is the y-coordinate
for point X?

A. +6   **B.** +3   **C.** −3   **D.** −6

15. Writing in Math Explain how to graph the ordered pair (−2, +3).

_____

_____

_____

_____

Graphing Equations

For each equation, find the values of y when x = ⁻1, when
x = 0, and when x = ⁺1. Then name the ordered pairs.

1. $y = x - 1$ _____ , _____ , _____

2. $y = 3x$ _____ , _____ , _____

3. $y = x + ⁻2$ _____ , _____ , _____

Graph the equation. First, make a table
using x-values of 0, ⁺1, and ⁺2.

4. $y = x + 4$

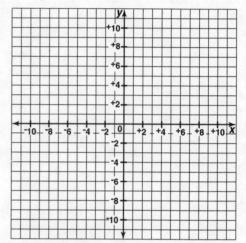

x	y

Bob earns $4 every week he takes out the trash. Use $y = 4x$,
where x is the number of times Bob takes out the trash, to find
how much Bob makes for taking out the trash.

5. How much will Bob have earned when he takes
out the trash for 6 weeks?   _____

Test Prep

6. Which ordered pair is a solution to the equation $y = 6x$?

   A. (0, 0)   **B.** (⁺6, ⁺1)   **C.** (⁺2, ⁺6)   **D.** (⁺6, 0)

7. Writing in Math Jolene says that the point (⁻2, ⁻1) is on the
same line as the points (0, 0) and (⁺2, ⁻1). Is she correct? Explain.

_____

_____

_____

Name_____

Equations and Graphs

Solve.

1. Today's high temperature was +15°F, and the low temperature was x degrees lower. If the low temperature was −5°F, how much less was the low temperature than the high temperature? Write an equation and solve it to find the answer.

   _____

   _____

2. Solve the problem $5x = 125$. Explain which property you needed to use.

   _____

   _____

   _____

   _____

3. Graph the points with ordered pairs $A(0, +3)$, $B(+3, -3)$, and $C(-3, -3)$. Connect the points and tell what type of figure is formed.

   _____

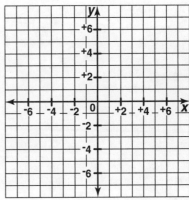

4. Martha saved the same amount of money every week for 52 weeks. At the end of the 52 weeks, she had saved $754. How much money did Martha save each week? Draw a picture and write an equation to solve.

   _____

   _____